John Hamlin Dewey

The Mystic key to Spiritual Illumination and Occult Mastery

John Hamlin Dewey

The Mystic key to Spiritual Illumination and Occult Mastery

ISBN/EAN: 9783337334796

Printed in Europe, USA, Canada, Australia, Japan

Cover: Foto ©Lupo / pixelio.de

More available books at **www.hansebooks.com**

THE MYSTIC KEY

TO

SPIRITUAL ILLUMINATION

AND

OCCULT MASTERY

BY

JOHN HAMLIN DEWEY, M.D.

AUTHOR OF "CHRISTIAN THEOSOPHY SERIES," ETC.

A CONDENSED COURSE OF LESSON HELPS FOR HOME STUDY AND PRACTICE IN PSYCHOMETRY, INTUITION, INSPIRATION, SEERSHIP, SPIRITUAL HEALING, ETC., IN CONNECTION WITH SPECIAL INSTRUCTION BY CORRESPONDENCE

PRINTED FOR THE AUTHOR

NOTICE.

Since the publication of "The Way, The Truth and The Life: a Handbook of Christian Theosophy, Healing and Psychic Culture," the author has received numerous applications for special instruction by mail. Not having time for the requisite correspondence, he has hitherto been obliged to refuse all such applications. Many of these calls, however, have been so urgent, that he has been led to devise a plan whereby he now can, with the aid of a carefully arranged series of Lesson-Helps, meet this demand, and is thus enabled to respond to those at a distance desiring his aid in their psychic and spiritual development.

These Lesson-Helps, Dr. Dewey has prepared especially for the correspondence course. They give in condensed form the essential facts and principles necessary for an understanding of the special lessons by correspondence, and make expeditious and successful the home study and practice.

Not being prepared for general use, each lesson will be adapted to the individual need of the student receiving it. The Lesson-Helps being designed for use only as a basis for the more specific instruction of the lessons by correspondence, they can be furnished only to those taking these lessons, and to Dr. Dewey's students who are qualified to use them in teaching.

The object being to help each student to such a degree of illumination that he may become a successful teacher and helper of others from his own inspiration and experience, he is expected to hold both the special lessons and Lesson-Helps as confidential; not giving them out, nor attempting to teach from them without the approval of

THE AUTHOR.

111 West Sixty-eighth Street, New York.

INTRODUCTORY.

An Open Secret of Transcendent Importance to Mankind, yet Apprehended by Few.

It is the secret of a stupendous truth, a truth so simple that it may be apprehended by the humblest mind, yet so mighty, when apprehended and applied, as to bring complete spiritual emancipation and enlightenment to the most benighted and depraved soul, and health and vigor to the most weakened and diseased body.

This truth gleams forth in all inspired teaching, but was first brought to its full revelation, in the perfect demonstration of practical experience in the life and work of the Christ.

It is the sublime yet simple truth that the power which regenerates, heals, illuminates, and brings to perfection, is spiritual and of God, not material or of man; a free gift impartially bestowed upon all who are in the attitude to receive it, independent of any question of merit. It is entirely a matter of understanding and motive, or of the proper attitude of mind and heart. "By grace are ye saved through faith; and that not of yourselves: it is the gift of God. Not of works lest any man should boast."

In forgetting their dependence upon God, men have sought through the practice of asceticism, and various devices of human wisdom and will-worship, to attain divine illumination; but "It is not in man that walketh to direct his steps." "Be not deceived, my beloved brethren. Every good gift and every perfect gift is from above, and cometh down from the Father of lights, with whom can be no variation, neither shadow that is cast by turning."

SPIRITUAL ILLUMINATION IS THE RESULT OF THE IMMEDIATE OPERATION OF THE DIVINE SPIRIT IN AND UPON THE HUMAN SPIRIT, SECURED BY THE CO-OPERATIVE DESIRE AND RECEPTIVE ATTITUDE OF THE INDIVIDUAL—the attitude of dependence, humility, and faith.

"In God we live, move, and have our being." All the processes of creation are the immediate result of the universal activity of the omnipresent life of God in nature. And these operations of the Divine Energy in the evolution or development and activities of life, are everywhere spontaneous up to the birth of man; that is, there is no power of self-determinate choice and volition in the kingdoms below man, whereby an individual plant or animal can voluntarily co-operate with the power of life to effect any given predetermined result in its own organism.

The processes of life throughout the physical world are, we repeat, spontaneous and automatic; but these spontaneous processes culminated in man; man being the ultimate product of the life of God in nature. This makes him potentially a reproduction of nature, and specifically a child of God. The potentialities of the universe and the very nature and attributes of the Eternal Father are focalized and engermed in his essential being. The further and higher evolution of life is, therefore, to be a spiritual evolution—the evolution of divine attributes and potencies in humanity itself. But with the coming forth of man as a spiritual being and child of God, came also a new and potent factor of life—the self-determinate factor of the human will.

The will, rooted in the personal life, of necessity co-operates with and intensifies the automatic processes of vitality in its own organism—God's life operating in that organism—or antagonizes, deranges, and depresses them.

What is thus true of the attitude of the will, or mind and heart, toward the processes of the life of God in the body, is even more vitally true concerning those of the soul.

The higher evolution of man as a moral and responsible being endowed with freedom of choice and action, is absolutely determined by his own attitude of will toward the Divine power that worketh in him.

THE SPIRIT OF GOD IT WILL THUS BE SEEN BECOMES SPECIFICALLY OPERATIVE IN AND UPON THE SPIRIT OF MAN, FOR HIS ILLUMINATION, ONLY THROUGH HIS ACTIVE CO-OPERATION—THE CO-OPERATION OF AN EARNEST DESIRE, WILL, AND FAITH. The mere passive desire and willing consent is not enough.

Absolute faith in God, the spirit of obedience to the law of divine unity and inspiration, and an all-absorbing desire after God, that will not stop short of full fruition, is the specific attitude which opens man, soul and body, to the regenerating or quickening and transforming operations of the Divine Spirit.

The awakening and exercise of this faith, spirit, desire, and attitude, is the preparatory and co-operative work which belongs to man. However long delayed, slow, and imperfect this work on his part may be, the immediate operation of Divine power in and upon the soul and body is unfailing, quick, and perfect, to the full extent of the individual co-operation.

Experience proves that in this work of preparation and co-operation, or of attaining and holding the proper attitude of mind and heart, the vast majority of people need the helping sympathy and counsel of such as have had personal experience in attainment.

The object of these Lesson-Helps, with the accompanying correspondence, is to open the understanding, touch the heart, awaken faith, and give the needed help to all who seek it at the author's hands.

A WORD TO THE STUDENT.—While pursuing this course of lessons, the student is expected to accept, provisionally, the fundamental statements presented, as the basis of interpretation; and not to modify the obvious meaning by any other standard.

It is of the first importance that teacher and student work from the basis of a common understanding, and put the same meaning into the expressions used.

Both the method adopted and the results aimed at and promised in the following course, are based upon the premises laid down, and unless all differing views and conceptions are put aside, and these accepted for the time as the working hypothesis, the course should not be entered upon. This condition is imperative.

THE BASIC CONCEPTION

THE NECESSARY STANDARD OF FAITH AND EFFORT.

1. Every thinking mind has some more or less clearly defined conception of that system of things of which we are a living part, and to which we are thus vitally related. A man's conception of God and the world determines his understanding of the nature of his relations to the laws of life and being, and so his attitude under these relations.

The nature and character of his basic conception is, therefore, a matter of fundamental importance, since it determines largely the character and results of all efforts at advancement.

2. The right attitude under the laws of life and being is necessary for perfect results; and this is possible only on the basis of a true conception of the constitution of things and of our relations thereto.

3. The conception or understanding which a man thus holds, determines his ideal of possible attainment; and this ideal will constitute both the basis and measure of his faith and effort.

4. We have the record of at least one of the human

race who had the true basis, and the attitude which opened to him the full freedom of the perfect life. This admitted, we have in him, "who is called Christ," the perfect Teacher and Exemplar for all.

5. The key to his successful interpretation and attitude, was his conception of God. God, to his understanding, was omniscient, omnipotent, and omnipresent Spirit, immanent in nature and man as the indwelling life of both, yet transcending the universe in and through which He is manifest, as the human spirit transcends the body.

6. Let us then unite on the basis of this Christ conception and interpretation, and through careful consideration seek to realize all that this fundamental postulate involves. In so doing, we too shall be enabled to take the attitude and secure the results which so distinguished the Master.

"GOD IS SPIRIT."

7. That in which the world and all things and beings are embosomed, upheld, and sustained, is Spirit.

8. The all-animating Life, creative Energy, sustaining Power, and directing Intelligence of the universe, is Spirit; and Spirit, in this conception, constitutes Original, Supreme, and Absolute Being.

9. To the luminous soul of the Master, God was not only above the world as transcendent, self-existent, and unconditioned Being, but was in His world as its life giving Spirit, clothing the grass of the field, feeding the fowls of the air, and holding the life and destiny of man and all things in the most bountiful and perfect providence.

THE MACROCOSM.

10. Recognizing all the processes of creation as the manifestation or activity of the living God in His world, we must regard the Universe as an organism in which Deific life and Divine power are regnant in every part.

11. This gives us then, for our basic conception, the Universe, which philosophers call the Macrocosm or great World, as an organism, of which man being a reproduction in miniature, is called the microcosm or little world—" In little all the sphere."

12. As an organism, the Universe or Macrocosm is threefold; corresponding with the body, soul, and spirit in man.

First, the outer physical world of materiality, form, and phenomena.

Second, the ethereal substance and constructive forces of the inner, occult world, which determine physical form and phenomena, and which, in organized activities, constitute the soul of the world; and in the infinite variety of individualized expression, "the soul of things."

Third, the innermost and transcendent realm of Universal, Impersonal, and Spiritual Being, the all-embracing sphere of the Divine and Absolute—the kingdom of God—in whose omnipresent Spirit all atoms, worlds, and beings are held in one united and perfect whole, giving to the universe a divine aim and purpose, and ordaining all things to the ends of wisdom and use.

13. That which is called substance, of which worlds and organisms are composed (both outer and inner), ex-

ists in infinite gradation from the state called crude matter, up to the most refined and subtile condition of impalpable ether. Within, behind, and above this, is that imparticled and Ineffable Essence or living Spirit, which constitutes the eternal and formless Substance of changeless and Absolute Being, in and by whom all things are.

14. On the one hand we have the substance of which worlds and organisms are produced, rising in gradation from the physical formations of the material world, up to the interior and ever-expanding zones of celestial spheres, and the ethereal forms of the spiritual beings which inhabit them; on the other hand we have the inner organizing forces, within and behind which is the omnipresent and creative Spirit that produces; the Divine Artisan and Director—all things being thus inter-related and one in Him.

15. The organic activities manifest in the processes of creation and providence, we call the soul of the world, of which the informing and controlling Spirit is God. All things, however seemingly insignificant in position and function, are, therefore, embraced in His eternal purpose and providence. "The eye cannot say unto the hand, I have no need of thee; nor again the hand to the feet, I have no need of you."

16. Each distinct element or compound has its distinguishing properties or characteristic attributes, derived immediately from God, which constitute its individual life and determining soul; thus it will be seen there is a soul of things, and of worlds, as well as of beings.

17. In the universe as an organism, every atom or combination of atoms is held in the all-penetrating and

all-embracing life of God; hence, while there is constant change and transformation going on in the processes of creation and dissolution, there is in reality no such thing as death. That which we call death is only a change in the relation of elements and forces, and applies to the disintegration of physical forms: never to spiritual organisms.

> "There is no Death! The dust we tread
> Shall change beneath the summer showers
> To golden grain or mellow fruit,
> Or rainbow-tinted flowers.
>
> "The granite rocks disorganize
> To feed the hungry moss they bear:
> The forest leaves drink daily life
> From out the viewless air."

In the dissolution of physical bodies and the transposition of material elements, we have the active manifestation of a living power. As the essential properties of matter, whether as primary elements or compound substances, are derived from the all-permeating and insphering life of God, there can be no positively dead or inert substance.

CONSCIOUSNESS, VS. SELF-CONSCIOUSNESS.

18. Consciousness being a specific property of soul-life, there must be a degree of consciousness attending the activity of every element, thing, or being. Self-consciousness, however, being the product of organized

and developed mentality, belongs only to self-determinate beings; hence, while consciousness is a universal attribute or condition of soul-life, self-consciousness is possible only to special conditions of soul-life.

19. In the order of evolution, man was the first form of life to come to self-consciousness, because the processes of creation culminating in him, make him a reproduction of the Macrocosm, and thus a self-determinate, self-conscious, and indestructible being and personality; a child of God, and, therefore, himself a god in embryo.

20. God, as we have seen, is the all in all of things, yet we must remember that the all of things do not constitute God. Spiritual, Infinite, and Absolute Being, He is infinitely more than the things and beings that exist in Him. "There is one God and Father of all, who is above all, and through all, and in you all."

21. It is in the transcendency of His Spiritual Being that God is the Father of human spirits; and it is as individualized and embodied spiritual beings—individualized through embodiment—that men are children of God.

22. This Christ-conception of the universe as an organism which God is both immanent in and transcendent over, and as such the Father of men, is fundamental and all-embracing; and should be dwelt upon until it becomes vital to us, as it was to the Master. It will then become the fulcrum of a mighty lever for the uplifting and expansion of the soul's life, consciousness, and powers, and thus outwork the most stupendous results in personal experience, as illustrated in our great Exem-

plar. That mighty lever is the correlative conception of man as a microcosm and thus a child of God.

MAN THE MICROCOSM.

23. Man, in this conception, is an epitome or reproduction in miniature of the threefold Macrocosm, each distinct sphere of which has its complete correspondence and representation in him. He is, therefore, as a microcosm something more than a child or miniature reproduction of what we call Nature, even as God the Father is more than Nature. He is specifically the child of God, a spiritual seed-germ of infinite possibilities, holding in the mysterious depths of his essential and indestructible being, the potentialities of the universe; the nature and attributes of the eternal Father.

24. It will thus be seen that our conception or understanding of the nature and character of God, necessarily determines our conception of the nature and possibilities of man as the child of God. This in turn gives our standard of possible attainment, and so constitutes the basis of individual faith and effort. It behooves each one, then, to give his basic conception the most profound and prayerful consideration, since that which he adopts will be the key to his individual attainment; because the necessary basis of his faith and effort. Men do not rise above, nor seek that which is above their own ideals.

25. If this Christ basis be the true one, we cannot possibly hold too high a conception of the essential nature and possibilities of man as a spiritual being and

child of God, nor of his inherent capacity for immediate divine realization and spiritual supremacy on earth. Let us then seriously consider the nature of these transcendent possibilities, and also the law and condition of their fruition on the firm basis of this conception.

26. First: Man as a microcosm, is a complete reproduction in miniature of the threefold Macrocosm. All the essential attributes of God, and the elemental forces and properties of His world, are focalized and represented in organic function and in their corresponding relations in his threefold being—body, soul, and spirit. The elements and harmonious movements of the physical world have their representation and correspondence in his body, the mighty occult powers and constructive forces of the inner world are organized in his soul; while the very nature, substance and attributes of Deity are focalized and engermed in his spirit. The integral development, or the unfolding and harmonious adjustment of all the powers of his complex being, will, therefore, bring all these to organic activity, and make him godlike in being and character, perfect even as his Father in heaven is perfect.

27. It is because the transcendental powers of his deeper spiritual nature have not been brought forth to their rightful organic activity and supremacy, that man has remained the imperfect being that he is.

28. The development and activity of the soul's powers on the plane of the senses, or in relation to the outward world through the senses, to the neglect of their corresponding activity on the spiritual plane in specific relation to God and the things of the Spirit, has led to ab-

sorption in the sensuous life, and that perversion of character, and dominance of the selfish spirit, that mystical writers call "the fall of man." The religions of the world have mostly been blind attempts to recover the lost balance. These misguided efforts have been based upon an imperfect understanding of the nature of man. The perfect way of this recovery, based upon the true understanding, was first presented by the Christ; and this has been grossly misapprehended and misapplied by the Church that bears his name.

29. From the incarnation of so much of the Divine Spirit as is differentiated and individualized through psychic and physical embodiment in man, his self-consciousness is evolved and the sense of personal identity established; first, on the external plane of sense-relation, and afterward on the interior and higher planes of the psychic and spiritual relations.

30. The informing, unitizing, and life-giving spirit in man, is the very Effluence of God, making his inmost and essential nature spiritual and divine, and holds potentially the attributes of the Godhead, with an inherent capacity for rising through unity with the Father into the full self-conscious realization of the God-life. But this unity with God must be the self-determined choice and act of man, in putting himself under the immediate influence of the Father's Spirit. He must will to do the Father's will, if he would know the reality and power of the God-life.

31. It is because the individualized spirit and personal life are the offspring of God, and exist within the all-embracing sphere of the infinite Father-Mother, that

unity of the human will with the Divine, is the necessary condition of rising into this realization. This fundamental truth has been insisted upon by all inspired teachers, and was especially emphasized by the Christ.

32. God as transcendent Spiritual Being is the supreme and absolute ruler of the Macrocosm, and so man, as the child of God, through unity with the Father, must and will become the absolute ruler of his own dependent organism, and of his environment; because this lifts him into the full self-conscious realization of the spiritual transcendency of his being. Careful reflection will make all this apparent and self-evident to every unbiased mind.

33. How this stupendous truth is to be grasped and practically applied, will best be seen by considering,

Second: That man, as a microcosm and threefold being, holds three specific and distinct spheres of relationship to the Macrocosm, differentiated each from the others by discrete degrees: an outer, an inner, and an inmost; making three corresponding planes of consciousness normal and legitimate to him—the sensuous, the psychical, and the spiritual.

34. On the sense plane, man is held in intimate and vital relation and communication with the outer and physical world through the body. Of this vital contact and relation he is made sensible or self-conscious by the activity of the five physical senses, or rather by the soul's activity in and through the physical organs of sense. The power of sensation and sense perception originate not in the organ, but in the soul that animates it.

35. On the interior or psychic plane, he is held through

his psychic organism in still more vital and intimate relation and communication with the inner occult world and soul of things. Of this interior relation and direct communication, he becomes self-conscious by the opening and exercise of the sixth or psychic sense, which, when fully developed and active, constitutes the psychometric or soul-measuring power.

36. On the inmost or spiritual plane of his being, man is held in the most interiorly vital and indestructible relation and communication with the very life and Being of God. Of this inmost and divine relationship and oneness of nature and life with the Father, he also becomes self-conscious through the opening and activity of the seventh or God-sense.

37. The opening of the seventh sense, and the development of the spiritual or God-consciousness, is wholly a matter of personal choice and volition, and is effected by the prayer of faith—the centering of attention and desire in confidence upon the Father—and by the final unreserved consecration of the personal will to the will of the Father. Man thus opens his life to the quickening vibrations of the Divine Spirit, and puts himself under its kindling and transforming power. He thereby co-operates with God in his life, and thus becomes self-centered in his own divinity as the child of God, and enters into self-conscious oneness of life with the Father.

38. When the spiritual consciousness is thus permanently established, the feeling of organic limitation imposed by the sense-consciousness is completely overcome in the realization of spiritual supremacy and freedom.

39. In this new sense of power and freedom born of the higher consciousness, the opening, development, and perfection of the psychometric sense and perception become a matter of easy and speedy achievement. If, however, this is attempted before attaining the spiritual consciousness, the sense of organic limitation and the bias of personal prejudice and desire will stand in the way of immediate and perfect results. The reason for this will be given further on; also an explanation of the nature of the sixth sense and the psychometric power—the grandest power of the soul.

40. Let us say in passing, however, that this spiritually quickened and sustained psychometric power enables man to enter at will into direct communication with the inner life of men and things, and read with unerring certainty their history, character, status and condition—moral and physical—and thus know them as he knows his own experiences. The secrets of the interior, occult, or soul-world, the actual states of men and things hidden from outward observation, become as direct and easy matters of perception and acquaintance through the psychometric power, as are the commonest things of external perception through the senses.

41. Very few are practically aware, or self-conscious, of these interior, transcendental powers and corresponding planes of relation to the Cosmos. Nevertheless, these relations exist and are vital to the soul, being established by the very process of individualization and embodiment through which man comes to self-conscious-

ness on the outer plane of the senses. He could not have been brought forth a microcosm without them; and because they exist and are vital, there is a corresponding interior consciousness attending them.

42. Man comes to self-consciousness on these higher planes, by the opening of the inner senses and the co-ordination of the self-consciousness of the outward man with the inner transcendental activities. The opening of these inner senses is effected, as already intimated, by the centering of attention and desire in confidence upon the things and interests of these higher planes, and is wholly a matter of self-determinate choice and action. Absorption in the things of the soul-world opens the sixth sense to the psychic plane of the mind's activity; and supreme desire after God and absorption in the things of the Spirit, opens the seventh sense to the kingdom of God, and the soul to the sphere of divine communion and fellowship.

43. There is a general consciousness attending all the activities of the personal life, whether on the physical, or interior, psychic, and spiritual planes; yet man is specifically self-conscious only on that plane upon which his attention and desires are for the time centered.

44. It is because the attention and desires are so fully centered upon and absorbed in the things of the sensuous life, that man is not self-conscious in the activities of the higher planes of his relationship. He is not yet awakened to the recognition of them and the vital activities they involve.

45. Self-consciousness being first spontaneously developed on the sense-plane, must be carried over to the

higher planes by the voluntary direction of attention and desire in faith, through the awakening of an interest in the things which belong to these planes. The higher activities and experiences are thus brought to self-realization, and become co-ordinated with the sense experiences of the external man; or rather those of the outer become co-ordinated with and interpreted by those of the inner and higher.

46. To enter confidently upon this work in the certainty of success, the attention must be fully aroused to these higher possibilities, the conviction of their reality fastened upon the mind, and an earnest desire awakened for their realization. This is best effected by a careful unbiased study of these higher relations and possibilities, as illustrated in the experience of those who have realized them.

47. Man must earnestly desire a thing before he can arouse his will to that degree of energy which compels the action or attitude necessary to secure it. Will is the expression of desire in an effort to secure the thing desired; and the energy of will is in proportion to the intensity of the desire which prompts the effort.

48. Before an earnest, persistent desire can be awakened for things above ordinary experience, a firm faith in their reality and desirability must be established. This accomplished, the focalization of attention in contemplation on the things of faith until their supreme importance is realized, will awaken the active desire and energy of will necessary to commit the whole man in confidence to the working of that divine power which

brings the realization. This is the needful work of preparation for all who would enter into this high experience.

"THE FIRST SHALL BE LAST AND THE LAST FIRST."

49. The spiritual plane should be the first sought and desired, because it is the central and highest, and when realized, subordinates and holds all activities to the law of the perfect life. When this is effected, and the external man and the sense-consciousness are fully adjusted to and co-ordinated with the spiritual consciousness, the sixth sense is spontaneously opened, and the soul becomes practically self-conscious on the three planes at once, and may then concentrate its activities on either plane at will. This requires perfect control of attention and desire, which is attained only through the permanent establishment of the spiritual consciousness.

50. Man is self-centered and permanently self-conscious only in that sphere of relations which hold the treasures of his heart, the attractions of which constitute the spring of his motives, ambitions, and incentives to action.

51. When, therefore, he becomes self-centered in God, and so in his own divinity, through the permanent establishment of the spiritual consciousness, all that is within him becomes subordinated thereto, and he is made self-conscious on the three planes of his relations, by their co-ordinated activities in his mind and heart. He is then at one with himself, at one with God, and so at one

with the world, men, and all things, in God. This is the true and normal life—the at-onement which the Christ came and wrought to establish.

52. Having contemplated God as Spiritual and Transcendent Being enthroned in and over the Macrocosm, and man as the child of God also a spiritual and transcendent being, enthroned in and over the microcosm, let us now consider the

OUTER AND INNER WORLDS,

and more specifically man's relation to each.

53. As the material world is external to the body, and its forms objective to sense-perception, so the soul world is exterior to the soul or psychic organism, and its contents also practically objective to the psychometric sense and perception. But the innermost and transcendent sphere or realm of Spirit—the Being and kingdom of God—is inward to the soul, the infinite within, and can be apprehended and realized only as such. "The kingdom of God cometh not with observation. Neither shall they say, Lo here! or, lo there! for, behold, the kingdom of God is within you."

54. The sphere of the Divine and Absolute must, to the individual soul, remain forever a subjective realm within, behind, and underneath, permeating yet inspheres all beings, things, and worlds.

55. God, and "the things of the Spirit of God," can never become objects of external perception, though they may be feebly represented to the spiritual vision in symbolic figures. They are known only through self-con-

scious union with them in spirit. They are to be inwardly realized, not externally perceived.

56. In the soul's self-conscious activity on the psychic plane, the psychometric act is twofold: first, that of inward feeling, second, of perception, though often, before the power is fully developed, the first factor only is realized.

57. On the spiritual plane, the soul enters into self-conscious communion and fellowship with God, by an inward realization through that supreme affection of the heart which yields all personal activity and desire to the sway of the Divine Love, and finds its full satisfaction in the realization of unity with the Father's will.

58. The physical senses open outwardly to nature and the external of things, and the psychometric sense to the inner side or soul of things, yet exterior to the soul itself; but the spiritual nature and its divine receptive seventh sense open inwardly to God, the infinite depths and heights of eternal and limitless Being.

59. While, therefore, the physical and occult worlds are the legitimate fields of human knowledge, activity, and achievement, and to be fully mastered, the kingdom of God is the ever within and transcendent, into which man can self-consciously enter and become active, only through the recognition of and glad subordination to the eternal supremacy of the Father's Being and government.

60. The spirit in man is the ground-work of his existence, and constitutes his essential being. By it he is inwardly united in the most vital and organic oneness with the life and Being of the Father. When through

reconciliation of will he becomes self-conscious of this union with God, it becomes the well-spring of eternal and incorruptible life, an unsealed fountain within the soul of perennial vigor and immortal youth, and, as externally expressed, an ever-unfolding power of knowledge, mastery, and achievement. "There is a spirit in man, and the inspiration of the Almighty giveth them understanding." God is ever giving Himself to, and working in and through the life of His child, to the degree with which the love and will of the child are one with His.

61. Man becomes self-conscious and self-centered in his own divinity by entering into voluntary unity of will with the Father, and centering his affections upon God and the things of the Spirit of God—the treasures of love and wisdom which that Spirit alone reveals. "Eye hath not seen, nor ear heard, neither hath it entered into the heart of man the things which God hath prepared for them that love him. But God hath revealed them unto us by his Spirit: for the Spirit searcheth all things, yea, the deep things of God." "The natural man receiveth not the things of the Spirit of God; for they are foolishness unto him; neither can he know them, because they are spiritually discerned."

62. Man is first individualized and becomes established in his own self-conscious personal identity, through his relations to and contact with other personalities and things, in a world external to himself. Hence, the physical and psychical worlds and his specific relations to them as an external environment, were a necessity to his individual existence; and for a field of

activity and achievement in the development and exercise of his powers and the perfection of his being as a personal identity.

63. When, however, his self-consciousness is awakened to the realization of his spiritual nature and immediate relationship with the All-Father, who is impersonal and universal Being, he is at once universalized in his sympathies. Under his relation as an individual to the external world of personalities and things, he becomes through unity with the Father, impersonal and impartial in his attitude toward them.

64. In the individualization and primary development of the personal ego in his self-conscious relations to the world of externals, before the spiritual consciousness is opened, man realizes only his own personality as distinct from, and in a sense opposed to, other personalities and things, and feels an interest in others only as they can be made to minister to his supposed necessities or pleasures. Such is the personal ego of the natural man, in contra-distinction to the impersonal ego of the spiritual man. The first is awakened and developed under the limitations and restraints of sense relations, and the laws of the animal life, which is *selfism*, in which as a personal ego man is self-centered; his own will and personal desire being the law of his life to the full extent of his ability to indulge them. The latter is awakened and enthroned in the freedom and supremacy of the spiritual life, by self-conscious unity and fellowship with the Father in the divine perfection and universality of his Being, in which as an impersonal ego, man becomes self centered; the Divine Will

and Purpose in all things being henceforth the law of his life.

65. It will thus be seen that specific personal relations and activities on both the physical and psychic planes, are a primary necessity, without which man could not have an individual existence; and that for the perpetuity of that existence in higher spheres, an external world of environment and personal relations will forever remain a necessity however ethereal and spiritualized that environment or sphere may be.

66. It will also be seen that self-conscious union with God and the realization of spiritual and impersonal being, while holding specific relations with personalities and things, is an equal necessity to the perfection of man as an individual; as by it he becomes self-centered in his own divinity, in conscious oneness with the Father, and so an impersonal ego going forth in impartial ministry and service.

67. The personal ego of the natural man must give place to the impersonal ego of the spiritual man, before the true and normal life of a son of God and brother of men can be realized on earth.

68. The Divine wisdom and goodness are thus clearly manifest in the necessary limitations with which the All-Father in His gracious providence has hedged about the activities of the personal ego and the selfish life.

69. Man is not ready for absolute freedom, or to be a law unto himself, until he is one with the spirit of all law and harmony, or in unity with the Divine will and purpose in all things. But, on the contrary, he cannot come into this unity with the Divine will and purpose—

the personal ego giving place to the impersonal ego—without entering into perfect freedom ; because he is not only one with the spirit of all law, but one with the Law-Giver in and over all things. He is then a law unto himself because the incarnation of law, order, and harmony.

70. The impersonal ego or twice-born individual, self-centered in his own divinity as a son of God, goes forth into the world to fulfil the Divine will and purpose in his relations to the world. By changing his position or center of motive from the personal to the impersonal ego, man has not thereby changed his relations to the world, but simply his attitude toward the world under these relations, by which he gains his victory over it. He is henceforth in the world, yet not of the world ; on the earth, yet above or master of its conditions. He dwells and moves among men morally above the power of temptation and sin, and physically above contagion and disease. He is held by this self-conscious oneness with the Divine and Absolute, above the power of all external conditions to disturb his peace and health in God ; and will no more be brought into bondage to any form of external condition or environment. Being self-consciously divine, the son of God in unity with the Father, he goes forth conquering and to conquer ; the master of life and destiny. Consciously the possessor and master of all things, in the Father, he goes forth not to be ministered unto but to minister, and give his life to the work of universal redemption.

71. This condition is reached by laying down all the activities and desires of the personal ego—denial of self—

that the will and purpose of the Father may be fulfilled, which is the governing motive of the impersonal ego, or of a soul at one with God in the realization of its own divine nature and sonship.

72. The call for this divine realization is never the demand of the personal ego, but the stirrings of the impersonal ego in response to the Father's voice in the soul, calling for the love and loyalty of His child, saying, "Son, daughter, give me thine heart."

73. The personal ego or natural man would, indeed, gladly accept and even seek union with divine power for the success of his own will, ambitions, and purposes; but the natural man never voluntarily and gladly lays these down, that the will of the Father may be fulfilled irrespective of all personal considerations. This is the attitude and motive of the impersonal ego or spiritual man, which, happily, lives deep down in *every human soul*, by which that soul is in its inner nature the child of God.

74. It is then in the power of everyone to respond to the divine call within, and will to be henceforth true and loyal to the Father, and thus co-operate with Him in outworking the royal destiny He has designed and provided for all His children.

75. For man to be one with the Father, and be guided by His wisdom, this must become the motive and incentive to every desire and act, since it is this only which constitutes that state of oneness.

76. In all mystical writings, the fall of angels and men from a state of innocence and holiness or unity with God, has been attributed to the setting up of the per-

sonal will and forgetting or ignoring dependence upon God.

77. There are but two centers of motive and inspiration possible to man. One is that of the personal ego whose center is self, and whose inspiration is self-love; the other, that of the impersonal ego whose center is God, and whose inspiration is the Father's love. The will is related equally to both; and the soul has the power of choice, and commits itself to either, at will. One seeks self-aggrandizement, the fulfilment of personal desire and ambition, even to the disadvantage of another's good; the other seeks to fulfil the Divine will and purpose, and under the inspiration of the Father's love, with his own, works impersonally and impartially for the good of all. It is from this center of motive and inspiration that all true mastery and divine achievement are accomplished. "Choose ye this day whom ye will serve."

78. All power of life is derived from the spirit within, from which all men draw for noble use, or misuse; but the limitation with which the activities of the personal ego are hedged in, prevents unlimited appropriation to evil ends. To the soul at one with God, seeking only to fulfil the Father's purpose, there is no limitation save that of the appropriating power. The supply is as limitless and exhaustless as the Being of God.

79. Men with favorable temperament, may, with concentration of effort, under a vaulting ambition, rise to eminence and distinction among men through development of mind power on both the sensuous and the psychic planes; but the limitations of human weakness attend all

such success, and sooner or later bring decay of power. All permanent achievement, true advancement, and enduring triumph come through unity with the Divine. True spiritual illumination and unerring guidance depend upon the opening of the spiritual consciousness; and this is effected only through self-conscious unity with the Father in will and purpose.

PSYCHOMETRY.

80. The external senses originate in the psychic organism, and have a psychic as well as physical power of action, hence are capable when closed externally, of being awakened to activity on the interior and psychic plane. Somnambulism, both natural and induced, is the demonstration of this. This interior activity once fully developed, however, both the psychic and physical sense functions may act in conjunction in the normal waking state, as thousands of experiments have proven, though in such cases the physical action is necessarily held in abeyance to the psychic.

81. The five senses, when thus opened internally, combine on the psychic plane in one all-inclusive analytic action which constitutes the sixth sense. This sixth or psychic sense will be perfect or imperfect, according as all the senses or only a portion of them are brought into full psychic activity at once. If there is introversion of sight only, we have clairvoyance; if of hearing, we have clair-audience; and so of each sense, and these results will be partial or complete according to the degree of development in their psychic action.

82. When all the senses are awakened to full psychic activity on the interior plane, they constitute in their combined action the psychometric or soul-measuring power. All imperfect exhibitions of this power are due to partial development in the subject. It has thus been spontaneously active in varying degrees of development in thousands, and may be cultivated to a reliable action in all.

83. This sixth sense, when fully established and its psychometric power developed, is the organic basis (under the soul's relation to the Divine and Spiritual) of intuition, inspiration, seership, and occult mastery, or "Spiritual Gifts."

84. The mere opening of the psychic sense, and the development and exercise of the psychometric power in and of itself, is but the focalization of the mind's activity on the interior and psychic plane, irrespective of the motive that prompts the action, and is not necessarily a step in a true spiritual development or divine realization. The psychic realm as well as the physical is external to the soul, and like the physical is a field for the exercise of the soul's powers, whatever be the motive. The spiritual plane, on the other hand, the sphere of divine communion and inspiration, opens inwardly and unites the soul with God in the fathomless depths and heights of its own spiritual being.

85. The opening of this sphere to self-consciousness is emphatically a question of motive; and is possible only through union with God, in the laying down of the personal will for the fulfilment of the Father's will; the personal ego of the natural man thus giving place to the

impersonal ego of the spiritual man, which is the true child of the Father.

86. Many have supposed that the development of the psychic powers, the various experiences of mediumship, etc., were evidences of some degree of spirituality, or development of the spiritual nature. It will be seen, however, that all this is possible without the first touch of true spirituality.

87. The activities of the personal ego may be pushed into the psychic realm through the cultivation of the sixth sense, and actual communication had with the souls of men in the body or out of the body, independent of the physical senses, as experience has abundantly proven. Nevertheless, all that is done from the standpoint and motives of the personal ego, is of the natural, not of the spiritual man, and is more or less subject to the bias of self-interest.

88. The question of motive is a moral, not an intellectual one. The whole matter lies between the standpoint and motives of the personal ego and those of the impersonal ego, between the standard of personal desire and ambition and that of the Divine will and purpose. Shall man go forth to develop his powers and seek to work out the problem of life and destiny in his own wisdom and strength, independent of a Divine plan and purpose in his existence? or shall he seek the guidance and fellowship of the Father in the fulfilment of that plan and purpose?

89. Ultimate victory or defeat depend upon his final answer to these vital questions.

90. If the attempt is made to open the sixth sense and

develop and exercise the psychometric power from the standpoint of the personal ego, the bias of personal desire, pre-impressions, hereditary and educational prejudice, etc., are certain to be projected into the result, and prevent the clear vision of truth. This is practically unavoidable to a greater or less degree.

91. The sense-consciousness of the personal ego being developed and educated under the limitations of strictly sense-relations, the recognition of personal limitation thus established is carried over to the psychic plane. This cripples the effort and prevents the full development and unbiased exercise of the psychometric power. Emancipation from this sense of organic limitation and the bias of selfism, which clings to the personal ego, is effected only through the opening of the spiritual consciousness and the coming forth of the impersonal ego of the spiritual man.

92. So long as motive and incentive to action are rooted in selfism, all efforts at psychic culture and occult mastery will be attended, more or less, by self-hypnotization and self-deception; and no perfectly reliable results are possible.

93. On the plane of the spiritual consciousness, all sense-limitations and standards are abolished, and from the standpoint of the impersonal ego, the love of truth for its own sake, is a quickening inspiration to the psychic and mental powers. The light of the spiritual consciousness and the confidence or conscious power it gives, liberates the psychic sense and exalts the psychometric perception to unfettered freedom and spontaneous activity.

94. From this standpoint only can the mind go forth unbiased in pursuit of truth, whether on the sense plane or on the psychic plane, seeking truth and right for their own sake, independent of any personal preference or consideration whatsoever.

95. Complete emancipation from the limitations of the sensuous life, and mastery of the outward world under sense relations, are assured only through the permanent enthronement of the spiritual consciousness by the opening of the seventh sense, and the development and activity of the psychic powers of the sixth sense under illumination from divine inspiration, by which they become the permanent gifts of the Spirit.

96. On the sensuous plane man learns from experience only, and develops his mental powers as he does his muscles, by the discipline of oft-repeated exercise in given channels of activity, and sometimes with slow and unsatisfactory results.

97. On the psychic plane, under the light and freedom of the spiritual consciousness, the soul learns by intuition and inspiration, anticipates experience, and perceives truth at first hand in whatever direction the desire and attention are turned. The spiritually liberated and illuminated psychometric power, penetrates with the quickness of thought to the very heart and life of whatever subject, person, or thing it is desirable or legitimate to know.

98. On the spiritual plane, "in the power of the Spirit," in self-conscious oneness with the Father, the soul needs to learn or acquire nothing. It knows and possesses all things legitimate to its state, even as God

knows and holds all things in His omniscient and omnipotent grasp. This is perfect illumination, and gives absolute power of mastery and possession. This is the function of spiritual being and divine realization, in which the physical as well as the psychic organism of the embodied spirit shares. Divine realization or perfect self-conscious union of the soul with God, is the realization of God-being, with corresponding power of God-doing. It is the complete realization of being and doing in God, and the Being and doing of God in us. The Father abiding in us—our consciousness—doeth his work. It is the omniscient and omnipotent Father revealing and giving Himself in His treasures of wisdom and knowledge, love and power, to the heart and mind of His child. "Son thou art ever with me, and all that is mine is thine."

THE ESOTERIC APPLICATION.

99. Having considered the fundamental basis and the essential definitions and discriminations involved in the points necessary to be grasped and held by the understanding, let us proceed to their practical application in the steps of induction, by which the soul must advance from the exoteric or intellectual apprehension, to the esoteric or spiritual realization in practical experience.

100. FIRST: the one essential thing to be kept uppermost in the thought is the supreme fact that life and the sustaining power of life are the immediate manifestation of God, immanent and transcendent, the all-animating

and all-embracing Spirit of the Universe. "In him we live and move and have our being."

101. SECOND : that the very substance of Deific Being —which is invisible and omnipotent Spirit—is the inner essential substance and groundwork of *our* being, as it is the primal substance and basis of all existences. Hence, as the outward universe is projected, formed, nourished, and upheld by the direct action of His omnipresent Spirit, each atom, molecule, being, and world receives its share of that sustaining Presence and Power.

102. The human soul, therefore, as the child of God, with its capacity for thought, affection, and limitless growth, and its organism for external activity and expression, cannot escape the omnipotent grasp of the Father's life, nor fall out of the embrace of his omniscient and infinite providence, love, and care. "Know ye not that ye are the temple of God and that the Spirit of God dwelleth in you?"

103. The recognition and realization of this stupendous truth is the first necessary step toward the opening up and practical realization of the interior life, in the power and permanent supremacy of the spiritual consciousness.

104. THIRD : that God, as immanent and transcendent Spirit and absolute Being, is the immediate Father of men. Man is therefore in his essential nature and being spiritual and divine, though individualized and differentiated from the infinite Father in personal identity and consciousness, by and through embodiment. Hence he, too, as a spiritual being and a child of God is not only immanent in, but transcendent over his physical organism and all his relations to environment through embodiment.

105. The recognition and realizing sense of this sublime truth leads the soul to seek and find in and through the transcendency of its own spiritual nature, direct communion and fellowship with the Father, which is the second step in bringing to actual experience the permanent consciousness of this divine supremacy.

106. FOURTH : whatever be the ultimate nature and origin of that which we call matter, there is not a movement or condition in the material world, minute or great, simple or complex, that does not originate in the direct action of omnipresent and omnipotent Spirit.

107. Spirit is the original fountain and groundwork of motion, life, sensation, intelligence, moral quality, love, and spirituality. Hence, when spirituality, whose law is love, has full organic expression in physical embodiment, all the preceding attributes and qualities become at once subordinated to this supreme law, and we have "the manifestation of the sons of God" in the flesh, in whom "dwelleth all the fulness of the God-head (God-nature) bodily."

108. Motion, life, sensation, and instinct were embodied and brought to organic expression in the kingdoms preceding man ; motion and chemical activity in the mineral world, life and vital activity in the vegetable, and these with sensation and instinct added in the animal.

109. The further evolution and embodiment of the still higher attributes of self-conscious intelligence and moral sense, conjoined with, but overruling all the qualities of previous embodiment, brought forth man, differentiated from and lifted above the animal kingdom, making of him a distinct type and higher order of being.

110. The specific attributes of reason, conscience, and aspiration, which distinguish man and differentiate him from all other forms of embodied life, are, as we have seen, the germs of divine qualities, with a capacity for endless development, in and through which the Deific nature—love and spirituality—become fully incarnate and manifest in the royal sons and daughters of the infinite Father-Mother.

111. All that is needed then to bring man to this perfection is the evolution and enthronement of love and spirituality as the controlling and directing power of the personal and social life. This, as already intimated, is to be effected by his co-operation with the Father's Spirit and power in his life, through unity of will and purpose with Him.

112. Co-operation with the Spirit and purpose of the Father, through unity of will in the direction of desire and faith, is the third and final step in attaining the attitude of mind and heart which constitutes the way of divine realization.

113. FIFTH: though a spiritual being and direct offspring of God, individualized through embodiment, man first awakens to the consciousness of personal identity as an individual holding definite relations to other beings and things, on the external plane, under the limitations of sense-relations and material conditions. But this, as we have seen, is only the primary condition necessary to his individualization as a personal identity. When this is fully accomplished and his self-consciousness and moral sense of personal responsibility is firmly established under these relations, he is ready to be awakened

to the consciousness of his spiritual nature and divine relationship, which is the second or spiritual birth. This follows as the immediate result of the attitude taken in the first three steps above mentioned.

"HOW CAN THESE THINGS BE?"

114. When this birth into a new and higher order and plane of life is first suggested to man in the sensuous understanding and experience he will say, with Nicodemus of old, "How can these things be?" Nevertheless he must be assured of the fact that he is in reality now the offspring of God, who is Spirit, that he is therefore an embodied spiritual being with an inherent capacity for inward communion with the Father, through which he will be brought to realize the quickening and transforming touch of the Father's Spirit, and lifted thereby into the freedom and supremacy of the spiritual life.

115. He must be taught that this second birth is but the awakening to the consciousness of his own spiritual nature, which brings the realization of the inherent divinity and transcendency of his being as the child of God, through loyalty to which he is enabled henceforth to dwell and walk in conscious unity and fellowship with the Father in all things.

116. This was the message of the Christ, which he enjoined upon his followers to proclaim to all the world, with the accompanying assurance, that whosoever accepted and entered into its mighty promise should be saved or brought to its divine realization in experience.

THE ONE SOURCE OF LIFE AND POWER.

117. The power of life and physical activity which is actualized by man on the external plane of sense-relations and the sense-consciousness are derived immediately from the indwelling spirit of God, which, as we have seen, is the primal and indestructible substance and groundwork of his being.

118. On the higher plane of the psychic relations and soul-consciousness, he realizes in like manner, from the same source, the power of thought and affection or of mental and emotional activity.

119. But when awakened to the inmost and transcendent plane of the spiritual consciousness, through which in his essential nature he is united to and one with the Father, he realizes the transcendent power of *being* and *mastery*.

120. Dwelling on the plane of the sense-consciousness, man is held to the limitation of sense-relations; because the standard of his faith and effort is born wholly of sense-experience. The power which seems born of the spiritual consciousness is latent in him as a spiritual being from the first; the conscious touch of the Divine and Absolute awakens him to the realization of it.

121. No new power is born in him from this experience. He is only awakened to the consciousness of that which was his from the first. It is not a question of development or attainment, but of realization. It is the heir entering into his inheritance as a birthright which he has done nothing to acquire, but which was provided and

bestowed as a free gift by the Father. Development or attainment is the law of the sense-life, not so of the spiritual; spiritual things must not be judged from the standards of sense.

122. This inward plane of man's being and relationship is as much a present fact, as is the external and sense-plane, and has been from the beginning of his individual career. The power of mastery of which he becomes conscious on the higher plane, was in him, though latent while yet under the sense of limitation from the recognition of sense-relations only.

123. The limitation he recognizes on both the physical and psychic planes is but a *sense* of limitation, which is only the limitation of his consciousness, born of experience under sense-relations; not a limitation of the power itself. The nature and the power are there and have constituted his deeper and true being from the first, only he has not yet awakened to the consciousness of the fact and actualized it in practical experience.

124. But having from the sense-plane attained the true attitude and thus entered upon the way, he has but to hold firmly to the attitude and understanding thus reached, and in the further recognition of the supreme truth of his being we are now considering, enter at once into its realization.

125. This higher realization is the exercise of our divine prerogative, in appropriating by faith or confidently taking up and exercising the power of spiritual supremacy which belongs to us as spiritual beings and children of God, and which is practically ours only by its appropriation and use.

126. This must be done, however, in the sense of unity with, dependence upon, and faith in the sustaining power of God. If attempted in the strength of our own will, we shall fail, for in this attitude we cannot escape the memory of sense-experience and the sense of limitation which that entails.

127. We must lay hold of the spiritual consciousness and the realization of power which it confers, in order to let go of the sense-consciousness and drop the recognition of limitation which that evokes. To effectually do this, we must turn from self and open our souls to God, in the confident recognition that He is our Father, and that we through unity of will and purpose with Him, as His children, have in Him the freedom and supremacy of our being. "Fight the good fight of faith, lay hold on eternal life." "For God hath not given us the spirit of fear, but of power, and of love, and of a sound mind."

128. To the full extent that we by faith lay hold in thought and desire on God and His eternal transcendency of life, His life and power take hold of us and we become consciously one with Him in them, and there is no longer place for the narrowness of self, or the limitations of sense.

129. Man can never know or practically realize his own true nature and capacity as an embodied spiritual being and child of God, until he becomes self-conscious on the three planes of his being and relations to the Macrocosm, in their co-ordinated activities, the spiritual or God-plane holding its normal and legitimate supremacy. Hence the Master says "Ye must be born again." "That which is born of the flesh is flesh; and that

which is born of the Spirit is spirit." "Verily, verily, I say unto thee, except a man be born of water and of the Spirit he cannot enter into the kingdom of God"—the kingdom of divine supremacy.

130. God is the supreme reality of the universe, and man's relation to God as His offspring is the supreme reality of his being, and this vital relation of God to men as Father to children, and of men to God as children to Parent, is as indestructible and absolute as are the nature of God and the human soul. And man must stand, or dwell and act in the full consciousness of this relation in practical experience, before he can know and exercise his normal and legitimate freedom and supremacy in and over his relations to that which is external to himself.

131. It is because he is practically conscious only of his sense and psychic relations that man feels his limitations under these relations. These relations in and of themselves awaken this sense of limited freedom and power.

132. But as God is within, behind, and above all these relations in the absolute freedom and supremacy of His Being, so man, as the child of God, when he awakes to the consciousness of this relation, comes into the practical realization of his own freedom and supremacy as a spiritual being.

133. Dwelling exclusively in the sensuous life gives the sense of limitation which holds man in subjection to external conditions, forgetful of his innate power of mastery; while dwelling on the plane of the spiritual life and consciousness gives the sense of spiritual being and

supremacy which brings its realization in practical experience.

134. It is through the absorption of attention that man dwells upon either of these planes; and the direction of attention is a matter of choice and volition.

135. If, then, as a living soul man centers his thought and desire upon the things of the sense-world, and seeks his wealth of knowledge and possession in that which ministers to his sense-life only, he necessarily becomes sensuous and materialistic in his thought and affection, and so dependent upon external relations and conditions. He thus comes into bondage to the very things he possesses or seeks to possess; and it is thus that mankind so easily become the slaves of sense, in bondage to "the lusts of the flesh, the lust of the eye, and the pride of life," which "are not of the Father."

136. If, again, man seeks knowledge and power through occult science and the cultivation and exercise of the psychic power of the sixth sense, from the standpoint of the personal ego, he carries the sense of limitation derived from experience under sense-relations, over into his psychical efforts by which they are crippled: and, blinded also by the bias of self-interest, he becomes more or less the subject of self-hypnotization and delusion.

137. But if he seek his knowledge and mastery through illumination from and conscious unity with God, he comes into the consciousness of his own spiritual being and supremacy, and is thus emancipated from the limitations of the sense-consciousness and the bias of self-interest.

138. Through the revelation or light of the Spirit of

God, in which the soul of things as well as the external of things are defined and held in their true position and relations, he sees and possesses their secrets even as God sees and possesses them. "For the Spirit searcheth [revealeth] all things, yea the deep things of God," and, "there is nothing covered that shall not be revealed; neither hid that shall not be known."

139. If, then, man center his thought and affection upon God and the things pertaining to the kingdom of God, the treasures of wisdom and goodness, knowledge and virtue, he becomes God-like in thinking and feeling, and thus impersonal and impartial, wise and good.

140. Through unity with God he enters into unity of spirit with all things, and both the soul of things and the body of things are seen in their true light, and appreciated for what they are, without exaggeration, deflection, or perversion. He sees and knows them as they exist in the mind and purpose of God, and thus has the absolute truth concerning them.

141. In this perception of and unity with the truth and spirit of all things with which man is specifically related, or to which his attention is called, they become to his consciousness essentially one with his own life, and so the legitimate objects of his love and care. He holds them in his mind and heart even as they are held by the Father.

142. Here, then, we have the infallible key to divine illumination and occult mastery, as presented by the Master: "Seek ye first the kingdom of God and his righteousness and all these things shall be added unto you."

143. Still, the question will be asked how to so seek that we may at once enter into this spiritual emancipation and realize here and now our freedom and mastery. To this there is but one answer, for there is but one way, and that way direct, quick, and infallible as illustrated in the Christ and Apostolic experience: "Ye shall seek me and find me when ye search for me with all your heart."

144. To break the power of self and sense, the thought, attention, and desire must for the time be centered exclusively upon GOD AND THE THINGS OF THE SPIRIT OF GOD, AS THE SUPREME OBJECTS OF DESIRE AND REALIZATION. These must be made the constant subject of the most earnest prayer, devout meditation, and absorbing contemplation.

145. When the attention is wholly centered upon any one object, it is to the same degree withdrawn from all others; so when the attention is thus fixed in confident desire upon God, as the All-Father to be realized and loved, the soul is thereby opened to the conscious touch of His Spirit, and this brings the divine assurance of sonship and oneness, the witness of His Spirit with our spirit, and the full deliverance, complete spiritual emancipation.

146. When this is once effected, the soul can go forth in its sense of unity with the Father to its activities on both the sense plane and the psychic plane, clad in the invincible panoply of the conscious power of mastery and achievement, and not again fall into bondage on the one plane, or delusion on the other.

147. There is but one source of possible danger of falling from this high estate and losing this power of mastery

over the external, and that is an over-self-confidence from an upspringing selfism and spiritual pride, which lets go of the sense of dependence upon the Father, and so loses the grace of humility, the only safeguard against egotism and spiritual pride, that pride which ever goeth before a fall.

148. Nevertheless, if from any cause, the divine light of the soul becomes at all obscured, and faith lets go her hold upon divine assurance, and the sense of weakness and limitation, anxiety and fear creep in, the soul having once found the way of deliverance and proved the Father's eternal and changeless grace, forgiveness, and healing, may again find prompt restoration by that way.

149. Any needy soul has but to touch the hem of the Divine garment of grace, in the spirit and attitude of a child, the spirit and attitude of love, trust, and loyalty, to receive the regenerating and purifying fire, the transforming and restoring power of the Father's changeless and quenchless love. His love is the transforming chemistry of the spiritual life, which transmutes by an immediate process, the basest elements and conditions of perverted humanity that may be brought under its direct influence, and remolds them after the pattern of the Divine ideal.

150. If we persistently fix our mind upon God in the contemplation of the spiritual perfection and transcendency of His Being, enthroned in and over His world in a gracious all-embracing love and providence, we immediately begin to feel the harmony of universal being, and the unshaken conviction that all things are indeed held in the secure grasp of His beneficent law, and over-

ruled and directed by His infinite wisdom and goodness. This sense of divine security gives birth to the feeling of confidence and trust, and the heart opens in glad and eager desire to be one with the Father in His wisdom and goodness, and in the harmony of His world.

151. This contemplation of God in His relation to the world, and to ourselves as His children, the special object of His love and providence—for whom indeed the worlds and all therein were made—and of our privilege of unity and fellowship with Him in these relations, cannot be entered into daily and persistently without enkindling and intensifying desire for this high fellowship and unity, until it becomes the all-absorbing passion of the heart and the all-engrossing thought of the mind.

152. When this stage is reached, the unity is effected: for the love of God as the compassionate Father-Mother, is realized in the very absorption of the child's heart in God. The soul's cry, "O my Father," is God's answer, "Here, my child." One is involved in the other, since it is the Father's nature in His child calling for its own.

153. This once actualized in experience, however long the time consumed in reaching it, the habit and the power are soon acquired of passing, in a moment, by an easy transition from the outer to the inner planes of communion, at will.

154. In thus withdrawing from outward things and retiring within, shutting out self and sense, and opening the heart in desire and faith for the conscious touch of the Father's Spirit and the revelation of His will, we necessarily place ourselves under the operation of His Spirit in and upon our own, and thus become a mirror for the

reflection or awakening of His image in us, and such revelation of His will as is needful to us.

155. In the passionate desire for and absorbing contemplation of an ideal perfection, especially if that ideal be to our mind a living reality, we necessarily become transformed into its likeness. This is a law of soul life. We do not transform it into our likeness, but are transformed by it.

156. So we cannot contemplate God in His divine supremacy and perfection as a living reality, and as our heavenly Father, without being lifted into unity with Him in the realization of our own divinity and spiritual supremacy, as His children.

157. Absorption in things of sense brings us into bondage, and under the law and limitation of the sense life. So absorption in God and the things of the Spirit of God, lifts us into the freedom and supremacy of the spiritual life, "The liberty of the glory of the children of God."

158. It was this divine law and certain method, to which the great Apostle referred in his second letter to the Corinthians. "We all, with unveiled face reflecting as a mirror the glory of the Lord, are transformed into the same image from glory to glory, even as from the Lord the Spirit." But we must unveil our faces unto God, by turning them from the things of sense and self, to Him, in desire and faith. (See in this connection paragraphs 37 to 51 inclusive.)

159. Men need to realize their dependence upon God for inspiration and power, spiritually, as they do their dependence upon nature for the sustenance which renews

the body, physically, and to give at least as much time and attention to corresponding seasons of spiritual refreshment as they do to the supply of the physical demands. When they seek and appropriate the wine and bread of heaven with the same confidence and eagerness that they do their earthly food, they will find an inexhaustible supply and the same freedom of access.

160. Of the external supply man may be robbed by his fellows, and his access to its source blocked in many ways; but no monopoly can in anyway be put upon his spiritual supply, and no man, no power of earth or hell can obstruct in the slightest degree his access to God. He has but to retire within, to the inner chamber of his own soul, to find the door which opens by his desire and faith, into the fulness of the Father's love and bounty.

161. Nothing, absolutely nothing can shut any man from this free, unlimited access to God, but his own fear and doubt. Let each soul, then, who would know this glad truth in personal experience, set apart a portion of each day for retirement from sensuous contact with the world, and enter into this free, unfettered communion with the Father.

162. In doing this, he should follow the specific instruction of the Master: "And when thou prayest, thou shalt not be as the hypocrites are: for they love to pray standing in the synagogue and in the corners of the street, that they may be seen of men. Verily I say unto you, They have their reward. But thou, when thou prayest, enter into thy closet [not only an inner room, or place of external seclusion, but the inner sanctuary of the soul], and when thou hast shut thy door [the door of sense],

pray to thy Father which is in secret; and thy Father which seeth in secret shall reward thee openly. But when ye pray, use not vain repetitions as the heathen do: for they think that they shall be heard for their much speaking. Be not ye therefore like unto them : for your heavenly Father knoweth what things ye have need of before ye ask him. After this manner therefore pray ye : Our Father which art in heaven, Hallowed be thy name. Thy kingdom come. Thy will be done on earth, as it is in heaven."

163. If these opening words of the model prayer be meditated upon till their significance is realized, the full secret of effectual prayer will be opened to the soul. That secret lies in the true attitude of the soul toward God. It is not only the recognition, but the realization of God as the compassionate Father of men, and their immediate source of dependence for all that they have, or may have. This fully realized awakens that precious sense of holy relation which the gracious words of the Master so fitly express, "Hallowed be thy name."

164. When this realizing sense of the Divine Paternity and providence is once established and active in the soul, the spontaneous expression of the heart's desire will ever and necessarily be, "Thy kingdom come and thy will be done on earth as it is in heaven."

165. The entire prayer defines and expresses the perfect attitude toward God as child to parent, which the Master everywhere emphasizes as necessary to entrance into the kingdom of God or the realization of the perfect and victorious life—the attitude of humble depend-

ence upon, trusting confidence in, and loving obedience to the infinite Father-Mother.

166. The fully awakened sense of dependence upon the All-Father and His perfect providence, establishes the confident assurance, which is "the rest of faith," that all our needs are not only known but provided for by Him, and that we may appropriate from His spiritual bounty as freely as we do from His physical providence.

167. In those words, "Use not vain repetitions as the heathen do: for they think that they shall be heard for their much speaking," etc., the Master evidently referred to the "yoga" practice of the Easterns, which consists (in part) of endless repetitions of certain specifically formulated phrases to which are attached a secret mystic significance revealed only to initiates.

168. The repeated utterance of these while holding the thought of their significance, constitutes a form of invocation which is supposed to awaken corresponding mental, or, as they are sometimes regarded, spiritual vibrations (vibrations upon the spiritual atmosphere) which react upon the subject to lift him gradually into the realization of the ideal of his desire.

169. This, it will be perceived, is, after all, but a form of will-worship in which the personal ego is really trying to answer his own prayers. It is a form of self-hypnotization which never brings the true, permanent realization. It is not based upon the recognition of a heavenly Father and a realizing sense of dependence upon Him who holds in His gracious providence a full and perfect supply for our every necessity, and to

whom we have but to open ourselves in this sense of dependence and trusting confidence, as child to parent, to have that need immediately and bountifully met. "Be ye not therefore [in your prayer] like unto them: for your Father knoweth what things ye have need of before ye ask Him."

170. If we are not anxious about this or that thing or supposed necessity, but seek only the fulfilment of the Father's will and providence toward us, "who knoweth what things we have need of," that which is best for us will be realized in its divine fulness. "Blessed are they which hunger and thirst after righteousness for they shall be filled." "Be not therefore anxious, saying, What shall we eat? or, What shall we drink? or, Wherewithal shall we be clothed? . . . for your heavenly Father knoweth that ye have need of all these things. But seek ye first His kingdom, and His righteousness, and all these things shall be added unto you."

171. Says Jacob Boehme, "the God-taught Philosopher," and wonderfully illuminated seer of spiritual things: "If the soul is to receive actual advantage and fruition from prayer, then must her will turn away from all creatures and terrestrial things and stand pure before God. Let not the flesh with its desires co-operate so that earthly desires may not be introduced into the divine effect in the soul.

Every prayer which does not find and take, is cold and insipid and is obstructed by temporal and terrestrial things; that is to say, the soul does not approach God in purity. She does not want to sacrifice herself entirely to God, but clings to terrestrial loves which hold her imprisoned so that she cannot attain the kingdom of God. . . .

Prayer is the union with God effected by the sacrifice of the personal will. It is, therefore, the only 'yoga practice' worthy of serious attention. . . .

He who truly prays co-operates with God internally, while externally he produces good fruit.

Mere word-prayer without exaltation of thought and divine desire (desire after divine things) is only an external thing, a mere repeating of words" ("Life and Writings of Boehme," by Franz Hartman).

172. It will thus be seen that true prayer and communion with God is effected and realized only by laying down or stilling all activities of the personal ego, or expressions of self-will, that the will of the Father may be revealed and executed in us.

173. This is the only possible coming to the Father, and this cannot be done without the immediate and full fruition of this divine realization in the unmistakable manifestation of the Father in us. His Spirit witnessing with our spirit that we are children of God. The conscious touch, and communion with His Spirit lifts us into the self-conscious realization of our own spiritual nature in its divine and rightful supremacy.

174. If, however, we seek union and communion with the Father for our own sake, we are still under the motives and inspiration of self-love, and deceive ourselves in the act. If we seek the Father for His sake, then in the very act and attitude of forgetting self for him is His love and emancipating power manifest in us. And we,

entering into His boundless and impartial love find ourselves loving all beings and things, including ourselves in Him, and as His.

175. But how can we thus forget ourselves in our search for God? Nothing can lead to this but the persistent and continually repeated effort in seeking to withdraw our attention and thoughts from ourselves and the things that pertain to self, by fixing them upon God in earnest and devout contemplation; to contemplate Him in the divine perfections of His being and supremacy, and especially in His beneficent character and relations to us as the Father of our spirits, and the provider of our every need or comfort.

176. Absorption in this contemplation will so touch the heart and sympathy with the loving qualities of His Being, that though at the first revelation we sink into the depths of humiliation at the recognition of the meanness, ingratitude, and absurd pride of our little self, we shall nevertheless be thus lifted out of all this by taking on the qualities we recognize and adore in the Father, and, awaking in His likeness, be satisfied.

177. In acquiring the art and habit of inward retirement for divine communion, some portion of each day should be sacredly dedicated to this object, and as perfect seclusion as possible should be secured from the noise and stir of those outward activities and associations in which the most of the world are entangled.

178. When this art of inward retirement is once fully mastered, however, no noise or stir of outward circumstance can prevent the soul from this high privilege and ineffable experience at any and all times.

179. But while acquiring this divine art, the greatest, yet in its true sense the simplest, retirement and seclusion as far as possible from the diverting demands of sense relations, seems to be a necessity to the still more inward retirement of the soul, and the holding of the attention and desires upon the divine and transcendent realities of the inner world.

180. Says Thomas Vaughan, a mystic of the middle centuries, in his "Magical Writings," "Now for thy study (meditation upon divine things), in the winter thy chamber is thy best residence. . . . In the summer, translate thyself to the fields, where all are green with the breath of God, and fresh with the powers of Heaven. Learn to refer all naturals to their spirituals by help of the secret analogy; for this is the way the magicians went and found out miracles. Many there are who bestow not their thoughts on God till the world fails them. . . . Do thou think on Him first, and He will speak to thy thoughts at last. Sometimes thou mayest walk in groves, which being full of majesty, will much advance the soul; sometimes by clear active rivers, for by such (say the mystic poets) Apollo contemplated. This is the way I would have thee walk in, if thou dost intend to be a solid Christian philosopher. Thou must, as Agrippa saith, 'live only to God and the angels; reject all things which are in opposition to heaven; otherwise thou canst have no communion with superiors.' Lastly, be single, not solitary. Avoid the multitude, as well of passions as persons. . . . To conclude, I would have thee know that every day is a year contracted, that every year is an extended day. Anticipate the year in the day, and lose not

a day in the year. Make use of indeterminate agents till thou canst find a determinate one. . . . Learn from thy errors to be infallible, from thy misfortunes to be constant. There is nothing stronger than perseverance, for it ends in miracles. I could tell thee more, but that were to puzzle thee. Learn this first, and thou mayst teach me the last."

181. There is no place like a mountain retreat or a depth of forest shade and stillness for a season of retirement, meditation, contemplation, and prayer. The great mystics and illuminati of the world have resorted thither, not only in the earlier stages of the divine initiation, but for seasons of spiritual refreshment in occasional brief retirement from the active ministry of service in contact with the world.

182. There is, in these majestic solitudes, an impressive stillness which serves to shut out the world of bustle, mart, and trade, hush to repose the feverish activities of the sense-life awakened by contact with that world, and woo the soul to meditation and communion with the invisible and interior things of the Spirit.

183. It is a great advantage, therefore, for the neophyte, in seeking to break the power of the sense-consciousness by the opening and enthronement of the spiritual, to improve every opportunity in using these retreats for their outward help to his inward retirement.

184. There is so much of God and His eternal calm expressed in the serene majesty and silence of the mountain and forest solitudes, that the soul once rising to full inward communion with the Father, finds it easy to recognize and walk with Him in the stillness of the

life which is active and manifest in tree and grass and flower.

185. In these experiences the soul readily learns its first lessons of holding conscious union with God in the things and relations of the external world, as a preparation for holding that consciousness in the more trying positions and relations of actual contact with men, and participation in the activities and obligations of society and business life.

186. In the summer time, as the mystic Vaughan says, we may greatly strengthen and advance our hold upon the interior life, and gain renewed power for service in the external, by frequent resort to mountain and forest retreats, as did the Master, and in the winters we may use for this purpose the seclusion and privacy of our own chamber.

187. But while thus considering the nature and steps of contemplation which lead up to permanent spiritual illumination, freedom, and supremacy, it is also necessary to impress the student with the fact that with the actual opening of the spiritual life and consciousness, and during the process of the co-ordination of the sense-consciousness, and sense-experience with the spiritual in its rightful supremacy, there comes a season of peculiar and powerful temptation.

188. It was thus with the Master, and has been so with all divinely illumined souls whose inner experiences have been recorded, and all with one accord forewarn and seek to guard the initiate against this subtle and unsuspected danger.

189. Temptation comes in the thousand ways in which the personal ego, rooted in selfism, seeks to maintain its

hold, and while seeming to yield, seeks to appropriate the new-born power and freedom to the ends of personal pride, ambition, or desire.

190. Jacob Boehme has especially emphasized this danger under which so many have fallen by the way. He says, "The enlightened children of God are threatened by a great danger; namely, in many of them who enjoyed the great sight of the holiness of God, wherein the triumph of life is obtained, carnal reason mirrors itself therein and seeks to intrude its selfishness into the centre from which the light shines. From this result miserable pride and self-conceit; and selfish reason—being, moreover, nothing but a reflection of the eternal light—fancies itself to be more than that. It thinks that it may do now as it pleases, and that, whatever it does, it is the will of God doing it in it, and it believes itself to be a prophet. Nevertheless it enters nowhere except within its own self, and moves within its own desire, whereby the *centrium natura* (personal ego) soon begins to arise. Then the devil of flattery comes forward, and man becomes drunk with self-conceit, persuading himself that it is God who compels him to act as he does. Thus he ruins the good beginning, during which the light of God began to shine within nature, and then the light of God departs from him. There is then nothing left but the light of external nature within, but self-assertion puts itself therein and fancies that it is the original light received from God." "Watch and pray," said the Master, that ye enter not into temptation: the spirit indeed is willing but the flesh is weak." "And what I say unto you I say unto all. Watch."

191. This seclusion from the whirl and activities of social and business or professional life, for contact with the unperverted life and undisturbed atmosphere of nature in the calm, quiet stillness of her solitudes, is a great help to those who can have it. We have nevertheless a still more important and effective help in association with those who are one with us in seeking the full realization of the spiritual life in its divine and permanent supremacy.

192. Union of souls in one ideal and purpose, and in associative action, creates a mental atmosphere, by the blending of their several emanative mental spheres, which reacts upon each with the full power of their blended thought, aspiration, and spiritual energy, and thus serves a twofold purpose: first, to quicken, intensify, and greatly reinforce the individual effort, and, second, to furnish a wall of protection, so to speak, around each member of the group, against the discordant and disturbing influences that may prevail in the world-seeking community in which they may be living.

193. Until the Brotherhood of the spiritual life is universally realized, local groups of those who have entered into a greater or less degree of realization, should be formed and faithfully attended, after the successful and victorious example of the Apostles just prior to the Pentecostal baptism, and in obedience to the last injunction and promise of the Master: "And, behold, I send the promise of my Father upon you: but tarry ye [continue] in the City of Jerusalem [City of peace, unity, concord] until ye be endued with power from on high." "And, being assembled together with them, commanded them

that they should not depart from Jerusalem, but wait for the promise of the Father, which, saith he, ye have heard of me; for John truly baptized with water; but ye shall be baptized with the Holy Spirit not many days hence." "And he said unto them, It is not for you to know the times or the seasons which the Father hath put in his own power. But ye shall receive power, after that the Holy Spirit is come upon you: and ye shall be witnesses unto me both in Jerusalem and in all Judea, and in Samaria, and unto the uttermost part of the earth."

194. These spiritual brotherhoods in their frequent gatherings constitute *our* city of Jerusalem, in which to continue and wait expectantly for the promise of the Father, until having reached the Apostolic condition, of being of one accord in one place, we too shall receive a like wonderful baptism and illumination of the Spirit, after which like them, we may go forth witnessing to the living Christ in the Apostolic power of ministry to the world.

195. This great injunction and promise of the Master should not be lost sight of, and we should continually seek for and expect nothing less, nor stop short of its full and perfect realization.

196. We have certainly an encouraging example in the first Disciples, who were no better qualified than ourselves (and probably not as well), either in capacity or education for this blessing, save in the one fact of their having been personal witnesses of the marvelous life and teaching of the Master as the basis of their faith.

197. But we have the essential teaching of the Master and the story of his life, as transmitted to us from them,

so that even this advantage is practically supplied if we fully accept the truth of their testimony, and are therefore without excuse if we do not act our faith and prove its truth and power in personal experience.

198. Still another aid, and of equal importance, is the earnest study of inspired Scripture, frequent prayerful meditation upon the words of spiritual wisdom that have been preserved to us of the great illuminated teachers of the world. Especially should we carefully study and meditate upon the life and teaching of the one supremely anointed Teacher, until we feel the touch of his mighty spirit and the kindling inspiration of his transcendent wisdom and goodness. "If ye continue in my words," he said, "then shall ye be my disciples indeed, and ye shall know the truth, and the truth shall make ye free."

199. Those who, from circumstances beyond their control, are deprived of the privileges of the association referred to, and perhaps of the summer retreat of forest and mountain, can at least enjoy this intimate association with the master minds and illuminati of the world whose words of inspired wisdom have providentially been preserved to us, and placed within reach of all people in civilized lands.

200. This wonderful aid to esoteric education and spiritual enlightenment should not be neglected, but should be an important factor in the associated work of the groups, and in the seasons of retirement and inward communings in nature's solitudes. The spirit of devout meditation, contemplation, and prayer is always more or less awakened by the earnest study of inspired writings, and this is a privilege within reach of all.

LESSON-HELPS. 57

201. Many modern seekers of esoteric wisdom lose much, very much, by neglecting the habitual study of the New Testament, forgetting that it holds the concentrated wisdom of all inspired writing, and the one complete illustration of the certain and perfect way for all. No other writing, ancient or modern, can compare with this or fill its place.

REVIEW, SUMMARY, AND CLOSING APPEAL.

202. In reviewing the ground over which we have passed in the preceding pages, what formulates itself to the mind as the true object of this esoteric study and effort? And what are the specific means and orderly steps of its realization as brought to light by the study? Let each student ask and answer these questions for himself, as in the closing paragraphs we seek to gather up the essential points involved, and bring them to the focus of a condensed and comprehensive statement.

203. It would seem plain enough that the real and only object or ideal of attainment and realization to hold before the mind and heart, is first, the opening of the spiritual consciousness, or the realization of conscious union and fellowship with God, in the light, freedom, and supremacy of the spiritual life; and second, the exercise of that freedom and supremacy, in unison with the Divine will, in and over all our relations to environment, on both the sense and psychic planes of activity. We are enjoined by the Christ to be perfect as the Father in heaven is perfect.

204. This divine realization should certainly be the

end and aim of all earthly ambition and seeking, because, as we have seen, it is the ideal, purpose, and provision of the All-Father for us as His children. We cannot therefore fully glorify Him in our bodies and spirits, which are His, by any less achievement. The first practical step, then, is the acceptance by faith of this transcendent possibility as the unquestioned purpose and provision of the Father, and then the unreserved committal of the whole soul to the work of its realization, not in our own wisdom and strength, but under the guiding inspiration and sustaining power of the Father's indwelling Spirit.

205. When this position or attitude of mind and heart is once fully taken, the next practical thing is to devote a portion of each day, however small, to the practice of withdrawing the attention, thought, and desire, from outward activities and the things of the sense-life, by centering them upon God and the higher life of divine communion and fellowship, in devout meditation, earnest prayer, and absorbing contemplation.

206. Few will find this an easy accomplishment at first, yet determined and persistent effort will bring success, and however prolonged, the divine result will prove it to have been a glorious investment of time and effort.

207. This daily exercise and consecrated effort should be unflinchingly persevered in until the perfect mastery of the attention is acquired, and the act of passing at will from the sensuous to the spiritual plane of thought and realization, becomes, as it surely will, an easy and cherished practice.

208. The spiritual power realized from this daily habit of divine communion, will sooner or later enable the soul

to bring the attention, thought, and desire under perfect control, and to direct them to the things of the outward or inward planes at will.

209. Special aids to this effort and practice, as already suggested, are found in seasons of retirement, seclusion, or solitude, as well as associative efforts of spiritual gatherings for divine communion and inspiration, and the special study of inspired Scriptures and the experiences of inspired lives.

The unbiased study of the higher nature and possibilities of man, in the light of the Christ life and teaching, and of the illustrative experiences of the seers and prophets of all time, is the best possible means of awakening and establishing the practical faith needed to lead the soul to give itself in unreserved co-operation with the Father in the work of realization.

210. There have been in all ages two classes of mystics seeking interior illumination, or communication and union with a super-sensuous plane of intelligence and power. One class have sought from the standpoint of religion, the other from that of science and philosophy.

211. These again have been subdivided each, practically, into two classes. One branch of the religious mystics have been most concerned in seeking the assurance of a continued and happy existence beyond the grave, the desire for personal salvation being the leading motive. The other, having less fear of the possible terrors of either annihilation or falling into realms of darkness and hopeless misery beyond, have sought for the enlightening wisdom to be derived through an inspiration from a diviner sphere, by which virtue and happiness should be

increased in the earth, human life purified, elevated, and prolonged, and a sure entrance into a better life beyond secured.

212. On the other hand, one class of the philosophical mystics have sought the higher knowledge and wisdom for the love of them, the desire for knowledge and power to solve the problem of existence and the mysteries of being, to become masters of the secrets of nature and the power of life, and if possible attain the mastery of death, being the propelling motive of their ardent search. The other class have sought the development of an occult science and magical art, by which they could wrest from nature her deepest secrets and acquire the mastery of her occult forces, as a miser seeks his gold, to selfish, personal, and sometimes diabolical ends. These have sought communication and alliance with the subtle intelligence and higher occult powers of invisible beings as a means of obtaining these ends; thus degrading their mystical pursuits to the perverse processes of necromancy and black magic.

213. That these various schools of mystics, each in their line, have attained transcendental results, whether to noble or ignoble ends, and in some instances of the most marvelous, and, as some would say, miraculous character, there can be no question to any mind who will give the subject a careful unbiased investigation.

214. Man's noblest powers may be perverted and directed to ignoble ends and purposes, of which we have daily witness; but this is only an added reason why we should cultivate, cherish, and put them to their legitimate use, the end for which they were bestowed.

215. The fact that God has planted these transcendental powers in the psychic and spiritual constitution of man, is His own warrant and command that we should cultivate, cherish, and put them to their legitimate use in the uplifting, expansion, and perfection of our personal and social life on earth. Only by so doing can we co-work with God and the Christ, in bringing to fulfilment in universal experience the millennial prophecies of all time.

216. It was the cultivation and exercise of the transcendental powers in their normal and legitimate channels of activity, that has given to the world its great seers and prophets, its God inspired and anointed teachers, and the one complete example of the perfect man. It was the perfect development and exercise of these powers that made him what he was, the Christ of God, the Exemplar of the perfect life or God's purpose and provision for all men as His children. From his divine altitude of experience and insight, he assures us that he is an example for all the world, and that whosoever follows his example shall "not walk in darkness"—the darkness of the carnal or sensuous understanding—"but shall have the light of life"—spiritual illumination—and shall do the works he did, and even greater.

217. The great Apostle also especially enjoins upon the Christian disciples, not to neglect the seeking and exercise of the transcendental gifts of the spiritual life. "Concerning spiritual gifts, brethren, I would not have you ignorant." "For to one is given by the Spirit [the "Divine Afflatus," or illumination from God] the word of wisdom ; to another the word of knowledge ; to an-

other faith; to another the gifts of healing; to another the working of miracles; to another prophecy; to another discerning of spirits; to another divers kinds of tongues; to another the interpretation of tongues. All these worketh that one and the self-same Spirit, dividing unto every man severally as he will." "But the manifestation of the Spirit is given to *every* man to profit withal."

218. With such examples and teaching we need not hesitate to seek the fullest realization of the divine promise made both in the gift of the powers, and in the assurance of inspired teaching concerning them. The noblest examples of human living have been the direct result of the development and exercise of these transcendental powers.

219. Ignorance of the nature of man, and the misconception of the character and function of these higher powers, resulting from this ignorance and the superstition it involves, and which has so universally prevailed since history began, has prevented the normal study and development of these great gifts, and so prevented the fruition of God's gracious purpose in them.

220. It is high time for men everywhere to awake from this spiritual lethargy and shake off the paralyzing incubus of traditional ignorance and superstition, and give themselves with a hearty interest to the study, development, and exercise of God's noblest gifts to them.

221. Men need first a proper understanding of the nature and function of the higher powers of the psychic and spiritual nature, of their true relations to the cosmos on the transcendental planes of being, and the knowledge

of a specific method of induction by which the soul may transfer at will its power of attention, consciousness, and mental action, from the objective plane of the sense-consciousness and relations to the interior and transcendental planes of direct communication with the occult world, or inner side and soul of things, and normal communion with higher spheres. All this we trust the earnest student will acquire, and be enabled to help others to, from the study through which we are passing in these pages, and correspondence lessons.

222. In the Appendix we give a brief and suggestive sketch of the "Science of Contemplation," as developed and practised by the founders and devotees of the monastic system of the Catholic Church, and its results in practical experience, which the student will find a profitable study. A digest of all the various methods of induction by which the different schools of mystics have sought to enter into the penetralia of things, and attain the higher wisdom, illumination, and mastery, will be given in No. 3, soon to be issued, of the "Christian Theosophy Series."

223. It will be found by a careful study and comparison of these different ideals, and methods of attainment and realization, that they all fell short of the perfect ideal and method of the Christ, as is demonstrated by the result in their own lives as compared with His experience. A tree is to be judged by its fruit.

224. The imperfect knowledge prevailing even among the majority of mystics concerning the spiritual nature and constitution of man, and of the character of the higher planes of consciousness and mental action possi-

ble and legitimate to him while in the body, was a hindrance to their success, and in most instances, greatly prolonged their efforts.

The proper discrimination between the psychic and spiritual planes of the sixth and seventh sense have rarely been made or seemingly understood. The confounding of these two distinct planes of relation and action has led to much confusion and perplexity of experience in seeking spiritual realization.

225. Most seekers have also, in greater or less degree, been misguided by the bias of misconception and the false notions of tradition and superstition, particularly among the Christian mystics. Yet, in spite of all this, very many reached the most marvelous attainments and experiences, approaching those of the Apostles, to the full extent that the Christ ideal and method were embraced.

226. The key to perfect results the Master has given, in seeking first Divine illumination, guidance, and help, through unity of will and spirit with the Father, which opens the spiritual consciousness (seventh or God-sense), emancipates from self and physical sense, and gives unfettered freedom of action also to the soul's powers on the psychic plane of the sixth sense.

227. Failure comes from attempting the attainment of occult mastery through the development and exercise of the psychic powers from the standpoint of the personal ego, by which the bias of self-interest and the standard of sense-experience are projected into the psychic efforts and vitiate the result.

228. This is avoided to a degree in the induction

by trance, which, when complete, shuts off the sense-consciousness, and thus prevents the impressions and prejudgments of sense-experience from affecting the mind's action on the psychic plane. The same is practically true also of the deeper ecstatic trance, when the mind being wholly disentangled from sense-relations and sense-impressions and the sense of limitation they impose, rises to the "third heaven" or central sphere, and is opened by intromission to the "holy of holies," the unveiled Shekinah of the Divine Presence—the "beatific vision."

229. This experience came to many of the Christian mystics, and has also come to some who, from abnormal conditions of disease, have fallen into the ecstatic trance and become for the time "as dead men." But in all these cases, as in the unshackled action of the mind's powers on the psychic plane of the sixth sense in somnambulism, this high experience was possible only from the complete closing of the external senses and the outward consciousness by the trance. This, however, is an abnormal condition in which the sense-nature is not subordinated to and co-ordinated with the higher spiritual consciousness and experience thus secured; but is only put to sleep, from which it is awakened unchanged and unaffected by the high subjective experience of the trance.

230. The normal opening of the spiritual consciousness is effected by voluntarily withdrawing the attention, thought, and desires from the things of the sense-life, and centering them upon God and spiritual things, in their Divine supremacy, which makes it necessary for the

personal ego to lay down self-will and the ambitions of selfism, that it may know God and realize the nature of the divine life, through unity with him.

231. But this requires the full waking consciousness of the mind and the free normal exercise of the personal will, choosing in perfect freedom to subordinate itself to the Father's will and become one with it. This voluntary, glad subordination of the personal will to the Divine will brings spontaneous co-ordination and union, or oneness, of the human with the Divine in all things. And just in proportion as the personal ego and self-will is laid down, the impersonal ego in the consciousness of divine sonship and oneness with the Father rises up. It is simply the voluntary unity of the personal will with the will of the All-Father, which transforms the personal ego into an impersonal ego, opens the spiritual consciousness, subordinates the sense-consciousness and activities to the higher law of the spiritual, and brings the whole outward man into unity with the inward life and spiritual nature in its divine supremacy. This alone casts out all bias of selfism, and emancipates the mind from the sense of limitation imposed by sense-relations, without at all changing the open, conscious relations of the soul to the sense-world.

232. Any attempt to seek divine illumination or the opening of the spiritual consciousness, which is the personal consciousness of divine sonship and oneness of life with the Father, without this adjustment of the personal will to the will of the Father, will forever fail. It is this alone that constitutes union with God, and voluntary union with Him is the only means of divine illumination,

which gives spiritual freedom, supremacy, and occult mastery.

233. It will thus be seen that induction by trance to the interior and higher planes of the soul's action and subjective experience, is abnormal, and does not in itself advance the personality one step in the divine life. This can be done only by the co-ordination of the outward with the inward man; the law of the Spirit bringing all things into unity with itself.

234. When the trance is induced by the help of an operator, as in mesmerism, hypnotism, etc., or again, as in the trance of mediumship, where the operator is an invisible or disembodied intelligence, the case is practically the same; this does not change the personal attitude toward God and the law of the spiritual life; besides, the mind of the subject, except in rare instances, is more or less under the deflection of the operator's mind, and perfect independent action is impossible. If, again, the sixth sense is first opened and the psychic powers awakened to their free action in the trance, and then, by a gradual process brought forward to the ordinary waking state, as has often been done, it is still found impossible to effect a perfect co-ordination of sense-perception and consciousness with those of the psychic, giving complete supremacy to the latter so as to avoid the possible delusions of self-hypnotization. The same old difficulty with the unregenerate personal ego rooted in selfism remains, and so long as this remains there can be *no unbiased* action of the mind.

235. Nothing but the opening of the spiritual consciousness and the enthronement of the law of the spirit-

ual life, can emancipate the soul and give the mind's powers unbiased and unfettered freedom of action on both the sensuous and the psychic planes.

236. Says Thomas Vaughan in his "Magical Writings," "She [the soul] hath several ways to break up house [overcome the limitations of sense], but her best is without disease. This is her mystical walk, an exit only to return. When she takes air at this door, it is without prejudice to her tenement." To which the translator and compiler, Prof. Arthur Edward Waite, adds, "This is an important and conspicuous instance of direct, though veiled, reference to the most exalted phenomena of the ecstatic trance, to which the common magnetic trance of modern psychology is scarcely the threshold or stepping-stone. The ancient mystics would appear to have discovered an arcane process for the elevation of hypnotism, by which the divine everlasting pneuma was joined for a period to the psyche or sensitive soul, and the spiritual correspondences of the subject were extended in an upward direction, so as to establish an ineffable intercourse with superior forms of substance. This condition of lucidity is unapproached by the operations of mesmerism, which are formed by the intervention, and influenced by the special characterization, of another human mind. Now, it must be established as a radical principle, from the true mystic standpoint, that elaboration of the arch-natural faculties in man can never be accomplished by this process. The creation of the Magus is personal in the strictest sense. 'Magnetism between two individuals,' says Eliphas Levi, '.is undoubtedly a marvellous discovery, but to create in one's self the mag-

netic condition, to induce one's own lucidity, and to direct one's own clairvoyance, is the perfection of magical art.'

"Those of impressional temperament, and especially women, who imagine, by the subjection of their individuality to a stronger and positive mind, to make progress in practical mysticism, should learn on the authority of practical mystics that they will not attain their end. Possibly the dangers of ordinary mesmerism in its other than healing branches, have been to some extent exaggerated, but it is not exaggeration to affirm that the many mansions of the mystic house of light are not to be discovered by the exploration of blind avenues."

237. The inward illumination to which Prof. Waite and the great mystic Levi refer, is, as we have shown, the immediate result of the conscious union of the soul with God in the inner depths and heights of its own inmost and spiritual nature. It is derived from no other source, and can be realized in no other way. The seeking of this illumination need not therefore be a work of many years, or months, or of days even, since it is a work not of the head but of the heart, a simple matter of choice and volition, a decisive act of will.

238. The "natural man" will ever seek to climb up to heaven some other way, but the one decisive question which confronts the soul on every hand, and which will forever rest with the individual soul to answer to and for itself, by which it determines its own destiny and experience, is this: Will you seek the doing of your own, or the Father's, will? The dominant attitude of the personal will toward God is our answer to this question, and our daily experience is the fruit of that answer.

239. Days, months, years, and a long life here and an age in the life beyond, may be spent before the soul is ready, like the returning prodigal, to lay down self and seek union with God in all things; but this decisive act *may* be performed in *this* life, *this* year, *this* month, *this* week, *this* day, and *this* hour, if we will. But let us be honest with ourselves and confess that when we are fairly brought face to face with this question, and it is pressed home to our individual conscience or moral sense, like the men of the parable we "all with one consent, begin to make excuse," and like Festus of old under the appeal of Paul, answer: "Go thy way for this time, when I have a more convenient season I will call for thee."

240. This is the practical question then for each student here and now to decide for himself, and on this decision rest the results of this present course of study. You are called to seek and enter into freedom, and, in the light of this experience, to help others into it; but how can you help others into that which you have not yourself?

241. In catching glimpses of these divine possibilities, men have eagerly sought a specific process of induction, by which the soul might enter into the immediate realization of its own spiritual life and power, and thus secure permanent illumination, freedom, and supremacy. The opening of the spiritual consciousness and its correlation with the sense-consciousness without the closing or suspension of the latter, is that specific process, and is the only process by which this experience is possible. But this co-ordination of the sense-consciousness with the spiritual, involves, as we have seen, the co-ordination also of the personal will with the Divine will, and is impos-

sible without it: for the ego of the spiritual consciousness is impersonal, the son of God in unity with the Father. "He that hath the Son hath life; and he that hath not the Son of God hath not life."

242. The consciousness to which man is thus awakened is the permanent sense of impersonal being, which lifts the soul above and out of the circle of the ambitions of self and all personal considerations, into the love of truth and right for their own sake, and the impartial attitude of universal sympathy, justice, and good will. This is the only standpoint from which the psychometric power can be put forth in the unbiased perception of truth, justice, and right, in which the mind takes on a purely intuitive action and perceives truth at first hand.

243. In voluntarily doing or seeking to do the Father's will, we do not by any means throw away or lose our own, but rather of our own free choice make it one with His, and thus secure its perfect action and guidance. This step once unreservedly taken, the soul enters into true freedom, and in self-conscious union with God finds illumination, guidance, and power.

244. The ability to subordinate at will the sense-perception and consciousness to the interior action of the psychometric power of the mind, in its unfettered freedom and supremacy, and the instantaneous and all-embracing grasp of its perception, is thus acquired, and the privilege is now open and free to all who will.

245. Let each and every human being understand that he is as directly and vitally related to the kingdom of God within, through the subjective or spiritual side of his nature, as he is with the outward world through his

sensuous nature and physical organism. Hence, he may and should be as fully awakened to and established in the self-consciousness of this divine relationship, as he is to his external relations through the senses.

246. This, as we have said, constitutes the second birth without which, the Master declares, no man can perceive, enter into, or realize the kingdom of God; yet this kingdom it was His gospel or good tidings to proclaim as at hand, or within reach and open to all. The condition of entrance into this transcendent experience, we repeat and reiterate, is wholly a matter of will, or of motive and attitude toward God. While the heart, or seat of the ruling motives of life, is to be reached partly, if not wholly, by appeals through the understanding, the real work to be done is with the will in the sphere of the heart and motives.

247. Man will never have the wisdom and power to so perfectly adjust himself to his relations with environment, as to secure the full fruition of his being in the realization of the exalted destiny designed and provided for him, until he is first adjusted by the proper attitude of will and motive to his higher and central relations with God. As these relations are of a purely moral and spiritual character, the work to be wrought is moral and spiritual, not intellectual and psychic.

248. The full fruition of man's being in his earthly existence is the entire perfection of his personal, social, and conjugal life, in which he is to gain and hold complete supremacy over the conditions of the outward world, and the entire mastery of environment. But this mastery of environment and perfection of life is confessedly

impossible without the perfect adjustment of the personal will and motive to the Divine will, as expressed in the unchanging law of universal harmony.

249. Man certainly has the ability to turn his attention and rouse his will in any direction he chooses. He has unquestioned freedom of choice and volition. He may not, indeed, effect at once the result aimed at in this direction, but if he resolve to persevere until he does, in the faith that he *will* succeed in the end, he will certainly triumph if the end sought be legitimate or in accord with the divine order. "He that willeth to do his will shall know," said the Master; shall know from experience. All the power of the universe is pledged by the very nature of God to the fulfilment of the Divine order and purpose in creation; every resolution and effort of man in the accord with that order receives, therefore, the re-inforcement and co-operation of the Divine will and power, and *must* succeed. "If God be for us, who can be against us?" The more fully our faith is grounded in this conviction, the more buoyant will be our hope and faith, and the more vigorous our will and effort.

250. That the perfect life on earth is attainable in this way, we have the unqualified assurance of the Master, and its practical demonstration in his life. "All things are possible to him that believeth."

251. The adjustment of the personal attitude in will, purpose, and action to the divine order, is a necessity to the integral development and harmonization of the individual and social life of man, and so of his rightful supremacy over all external conditions of environment. Hence the emphasis the Master put upon the first step

in the new education which holds the divine promise of such stupendous results for him. "Seek ye first the kingdom," etc., "and all these things shall be added."

252. There is nothing arbitrary in this condition of attainment, nor in its injunction by the Master. It is legitimate and normal to the very nature and constitution of things in which all the great doctrines of the Master's teaching were based. There certainly is no more compromise of the personal freedom of choice and action, in this adjustment of the soul to the kingdom of God, in our moral and spiritual relations, than there is in the external adjustment to our physical relations.

253. The sailor adjusts his vessel to the movements of the wind and tide, that he may utilize their power to the furtherance of his ends, and has the legitimate exercise of his personal freedom in the act. So with all the great forces of the physical world; man is enabled to utilize them by adjusting himself to the law of their action.

254. The most sensuous and selfish mind recognizes this necessity, and complies with it on the physical plane without thought of compromise to his personal liberty in the act, or of anything arbitrary, irrational, or unjust in the necessity. Indeed, man finds his normal life and freedom in and under these relations to the physical world only through his perfect adjustment to them, and wisely exercises his personal rights and freedom in the very act of adjustment. Nor can he thus cheerfully adjust himself to these relations in the spirit of reconciliation with them, without thereby securing his freedom, health, success, and happiness in them, because they

were ordained in infinite wisdom and beneficence to this end.

255. The recognition of God in and over His world, in the infinite wisdom and goodness of His economy, will give this spirit of reconciliation and cheerful conformity therewith. This principle holds equally true of every sphere of man's relations to the cosmos, and of his attitude in and under them. He has, therefore, but to really perceive and understand his moral and spiritual relations to God from the central and highest plane of his being, to find the supreme motive for seeking at once to adjust himself in reconciliation of will and attitude to these divine and all-important relations. Nor can he thus adjust himself to this central and highest sphere, without bringing his whole personal life under the direct and immediate inspiration and perfecting influence of the divine wisdom and goodness.

256. The difficulty is, and ever has been, that few have realized or understood their own spiritual nature, and through it their specific relations to the Divine and Absolute, and the immediate, stupendous possibilities these involve. The teachers themselves have too often been "blind leaders of the blind."

257. One finds freedom, fellowship, and delight in familiar intercourse with men, only through the proper adjustment of his own will and attitude to his true relations with them. So he will find the spiritual freedom, supremacy, illumination, and moral perfection of his being, in constant communion and fellowship with God as Father, only through the recognition and glad adjustment of himself to these relations as child to Parent.

"Verily I say unto you, whosoever shall not receive the kingdom of God as a little child shall in no wise enter therein."

258. There is but one motive which prompts the majority of men to seek to adjust themselves to their physical relations and conditions, and that is the personal good to be derived therefrom; considerations of pure selfism.

259. There may, however, be two different motives prompting men to seek to know and to do the will of God. The first would be the recognition of that will as involving the perfect, or at least the best way of reaching the highest results, and this without any special reverence for God. The second would be prompted by the glad recognition and love of God as the All-Father, and the realizing sense of the royalty and divinity of his own nature as a child of God, which leads to spontaneous loyalty, and desire to be at-one with Him for His Own sake, because He *is* the Father and *Himself* the supreme good.

260. The first is a prudential, and essentially a selfish, motive, yet even this, when faithfully followed, leads, through experience, to the final awakening of the second, which is wholly above the selfish spirit. Under the first motive, gratitude is awakened by the final recognition of the Divine goodness; from this in turn is awakened love; then comes at-onement in spirit, and with this illumination spiritual freedom, supremacy, and organic perfection.

261. In this unreserved giving of himself to the Father's perfect will and way, man does not lose, but gains,

and in no other way can gain his perfect freedom, supremacy, and perfection of being in and over all his relations to environment. And when this consecration is prompted by the supreme and spontaneous love of the heart, as it sooner or later will be, he will find therein the divinest joy and beatific experience possible to his being.

262. Two spiritually awakened souls united in the inexpressible felicity of a genuine conjugal affection, find their supreme delight and deepest joy in living in and for each other, and count no personal sacrifice too great to advance the other's good, and find exaltation therein because it is a service of love. So in the subordination of the personal will to the will of the Father from the love and adoration of the heart, there is no servile attitude or sense of arbitrary humiliation and loss of personal freedom, but of emancipation and divinest exaltation in the act. Indeed, the ineffable bliss experienced by mated souls when brought to the full realization of their inseparable union, is the one only experience, under strictly human relations, which fitly symbolizes or at all represents that divine sense of unutterable joy and inextinguishable blessedness found in the conscious union of the soul with God.

263. To awaken that love of God which leads to this holy union with and beatific experience in Him, we have but to take and hold the attitude of loyal children, and, as especially emphasized in these pages, persistently contemplate Him in the divine perfection of His Fatherhood, love, and providence, until this vision of God

becomes, as it sooner or later will, the supreme reality or beatific vision of the soul.

> " I cannot hide that some have striven,
> Achieving calm, to whom was given
> The joy that mixes man with heaven.
>
> Who, rowing hard against the stream,
> Saw golden gates of Eden gleam,
> And did not dream it was a dream.
>
> But looking upward, full of grace,
> They prayed, and from a happy place,
> God's glory smote them on the face."

APPENDIX.

A STUDY OF THE MYSTICS.

THE SCIENCE OF CONTEMPLATION AND STUDY, OR THE METHOD OF ATTAINING SPIRITUAL ILLUMINATION AND MENTAL ENLIGHTENMENT, AS DEVELOPED AND APPLIED BY THE MYSTIC FATHERS OF THE EARLY CHURCH.

Taken from "The Life and Labors of St. Thomas of Aquin, by the most Rev. Bede Vaughan." (Catholic Publication.)

To gaze steadily and fixedly upon an object, and take it in—to become one with it by contemplation, has a profound effect upon the soul. If the object be pure and elevating, the soul through its influence will be purer and nobler than before.

To look upon an object in order to analyze its parts, to compare and divide, to balance and weigh it, and to pass it through a process of sifting and manipulation, possesses also its special charm ; but it is the charm not of subjection, but of mastery, not of repose, but of activity. Some minds—according to the mould in which they are cast—have more natural sympathy with the first, others with the second, method. Each is good within its own sphere, both are pernicious when they outstep their sphere. Both are necessary for the perfection of the human mind. For man has a will to love and an intelligence to know. He can fix himself on an object in faith ; or probe and analyze it with his reason. . . . *Quies* is monastic ; inquisitiveness is dialectical. . . .

The Fathers, in their cast of mind, were essentially monastic ; indeed, the monastic system has been a traditionary one in the Church from the earliest ages, and rests upon two fundamental facts, studied by all deeply thinking minds, viz.: first, that Christ—who taught a Divine philosophy as well as a Divine theology—has never said "Blessed are they that see and then believe," but "Blessed are they who have not seen;" and again, "Love is the fulfilling of the law." Man's primary scope is, not to know, but to love; not to see, but to believe. Belief, and love, these are the two master-passions of all monastic minds—looking up with confidence, crying out "My Lord and my God," and then with all the passion of the soul embracing the sovereign good. . . .

The solitaires of China and of India, the Chaldean and the Egyptian, sought after a higher goodness and truth than they found within themselves; they sought caves and mournful solitudes, that they might undisturbed, commune with the Great Spirit of the skies. . . .

In the West, of which I am now speaking, St. Benedict was the first and only legislator of monasticism. He saw the immense force of the religious life of the East, such as it was. He reorganized it, putting it on a more practical and more perfect footing. The Easterns buried themselves in solitudes, there to remain and converse with God; St. Benedict had humanity in view: he hurried to the rugged fastness, to live to God, and having lived to God, to come forth and subdue the world, through the synthetic influence of the cross. His system is written in what, *par excellence*, is called "The Holy Rule:" a rule which St. Gregory, St. Thomas, and others declare to have been immediately inspired by the Holy Ghost. Its whole scope demonstrates that St. Benedict held that "love" was power. . . . He found love in the mountain cave. . . . Love is not the offspring of analyzing, and dividing, and arguing, but it is the child of contemplation, and peace. How is this love acquired? The Holy Rule lays down the method. Love is acquired by two things, viz., by contemplation, and by purity of heart. He who has a pure heart and contemplates truth, loves truth. The contemplation will be clear in proportion as the heart is pure, and the heart will be pure as the spirit is humble.

Dependence upon God as the Father, and yielding the personal will to His in perfect trust of His infinite wisdom and goodness is the law.

The two grand principles on which that Rule—which has given its color to every other—is founded, are the contemplation of love and the

APPENDIX.   81

practice of humility. But what is the object of contemplation ? The
object is Christ. [It should be remembered that Christ is here regarded
by St. Benedict and all the Mystic Fathers as God incarnate as the
Saviour of men, hence Christ to their thought stood as the objective im-
personation of love.] Christ seems incarnate in this Rule. . . .
Christ is seen in the sick; Christ is served in the guests. The monk is
"to deny himself to himself and follow Christ." The community is all
one in Christ; and the Holy Legislator insists that nothing is to be
placed before the love of Christ. . . .

Now, it is self-evident that, in proportion as the soul contemplates
Christ, and the heart is pure, the will elicits perfect acts of love. Again,
in relation of man to his Maker, there is always a disproportion, which
becomes more evident as he advances in love and purity of heart. In
the same degree as the creature knows what the Creator is, he realizes
his own position as a creature. . . . What then do we call the result in the mind of the realization of this proportion ? Surely, Reverence. The love man has for God is an adoring love. Love, reverence,
adoration, purity—these are the four pillars of the grand monastic
system. Those who were real monks were thoroughly possessed by
these gifts They created the atmosphere [mental] in which they lived,
and consequently in which they thought. They formed the character
of the man and the temper of his mind, and monks could no more
think independently of their influence than we can think outside the
grooves of space and time. . . .

St. Bernard was the great founder of the monastic method. . . .
Bernard was scholastic, but he was pre-eminently contemplative. . . .

The tendency of St. Bernard's mind is evident from the subject
matter of his most important works. His treatise on grace and free
will; his book on contemplation; his writings on the love of God;
and then his tract on the degrees of humility, all point to the one object which possessed his mind. Love and faith, purity and humility,
these make up all the strivings and aspirations of St. Bernard's life.
. . . In fact his treatise on grace is simply a preparation for his
treatise on the love of God. Here Bernard is evidently in his element.
The cause of our loving God is God himself; the measure of love is to
love without measure. The very voice of nature within man loudly
calls upon him to love God. Love is not mercenary ["seeketh not her
own"]. Love is the reward of love. Love is not attained at once.

There are four steps to perfect love: It begins with self; next, man loves God selfishly; then he loves him unselfishly—for His own sake; and lastly, he loves not God alone for His own sake; but he loves himself and all other things for the love of God. That is the highest perfection of Divine love. But the fullest perfection of this form is only then experienced, when the soul, for the moment, is carried by mystical rapture as it were beyond itself.

But love cannot be treated without touching upon its counterpart—humility. What purity of heart was to St. Anselm, that humility was to St. Bernard. These great, pure minded thinkers laid the principal stress on that which seems to be almost entirely disregarded at this day. It was evident to them that the soul could not contemplate truth if its eye—the heart—were not clean, as it is to us that we cannot see when our eyes are shut. They saw distinctly what we forget, or ignore, viz.: the intimate connection, more intimate than that of body and soul, between the intellectual and moral faculties—between the intelligence and will.

Humility is the virtue, says the Saint, by which a man looks meanly upon himself, through a perfectly accurate appreciation of himself. This is the way to knowledge. There are twelve degrees before man arrives at the full blaze of enlightening truth. But he declares that humility is not enough. In order to possess the highest form of knowledge, love must be added to humility. When man has arrived at the highest form of life through love and humility, then he begins to enter into the mystic region. The first step here is consideration, which is an intense application of the mind acting discursively upon some given truth. The next is contemplation, which passing beyond the discursive action of the reason, rests fixed intently on the object. The effect of contemplation is to produce admiration and wonder; so much so that, being overcome by the power of the majesty before it, the spirit is lifted, as it were, out of itself, and for the time is plunged in the ocean of illimitable truth. As a drop of water falling into wine seems to become wine, taking its taste and color; . . . as the air penetrated with light seems to become an illumination, and no longer air; so in the other world [the ecstatic state], will the soul be carried away with God. For the creature thus possessed of God marvellously forgets itself, and, altogether leaving self, wholly goes to God, and from henceforth adhering to Him, becomes one spirit with Him.

APPENDIX. 83

Richard of St. Victor's, a Scotchman, like many other students of this epoch, . . . came to Paris, attracted by the fame of the schools. He entered at St. Victor's and was professed under the first Abbot, Guilduin. . . . What is particularly aimed at here, is to give an outline of his mystic teaching regarding the methods of contemplation, not merely because he brought to its fulness that which St. Bernard and Hugh had labored at before him, but because to appreciate the moral and ecstatic life of St. Thomas of Aquin, some knowledge of the relations of the mind with contemplation and spiritual intuition is requisite. . . .

His first principles regarding knowledge are identical with those of the holy men that went before him. Faith comes first. If we do not believe we cannot understand; knowledge must enter by faith; it must not indeed rest in the entrance, for it should *always* hasten on to interior and profound things, and by earnest study and diligence seek to advance daily in the understanding of those things which we hold by faith: these are the best riches—these are the eternal delights. Again, the first study of a manly mind ought to be how to govern its affections, and the second, how to command its thoughts. . . .

Before treating of Richard's theory of contemplation, a word must be said of his view of the human soul. He starts with the assumption that the soul is a simple substance, which gives life and sensibility to the body. He divides the spiritual portion into spirit and soul, according to the more or less elevated attributes belonging to each. Every reasonable man possesses two gifts—one of reason, by which he knows; another of affection, with which he loves. Reason points to truth; affection to virtue. . . . Considered in their relation to the object, our faculties are threefold: The imagination, the reason, and the intelligence [intuition]. The reason stands between the imagination and the intelligence. The office of the imagination is to seize and hold sensible impressions, the reason is the instrument of discursive thought, by which we advance, by way of premise and conclusion, toward the truth. The intelligence [intuition] is a still higher power which, as the senses seize, by immediate apprehension, their proper objects, grasps, in an immediate manner, its proper object. The intelligence is pure, inasmuch as it excludes the imagination; and simple, inasmuch as it excludes processes of reasoning.

Now to these three powers of the soul, correspond three methods of knowledge: thought, meditation, and contemplation. . . . Thought comes from the imagination; meditation from the reason; and contemplation from the intelligence. Thought wanders about here and there, without direction, slowly, as at will; meditation, with great labor of the soul, strives, by hard and difficult ways, toward the given end; contemplation is carried, with freedom and great facility, wherever the power bears it, to its proper object. Contemplation is seeing truth pure and naked, without any cloud or shade standing in the way [pure intuition]. . . . The foundation of the contemplative life consists first in the practice of virtue. The heart must be pure if a man wishes to see God. It is the old method of monasticism, which runs through the hearts and minds of the learned saints of God. . . . The second foundation-stone of the mystic life is self-knowledge. In fact, love and humility, according to the monastic principles of the "Holy Rule," are the two bases of the whole fabric of the spiritual life. The soul is a mirror, in which the picture of God's glory and beauty loves most to reflect itself, and in which, in a particular way, we can see and know Him. The soul was created to the likeness of God; and if His mark is seen in nature, how much more in that spirit which was created after the image of Himself. Hence, if a man would wish to contemplate God, he must purify and cleanse this mirror by his efforts after virtue and moral perfection. . . . ["Blessed are the pure in heart, for they shall see God."]

God is the proper object of contemplation; but the soul can also fix itself upon other objects. According to the subject matter, there are six steps of contemplation. The first is in, and according to, the imagination. This looks upon the beauty and variety of creation, and thus is drawn to wonder at and honor the wisdom and goodness of God. The second is in the imagination, and according to reason. This marvels at and considers the causes of the world of sense "according to reason," because the conclusions of reason are necessary for proceeding from cause to effect.

The third is in reason, and according to imagination. Here we conclude from the facts of sensible nature to the world of ideas, which are brought before the intelligence. "In reason," because the reason alone can move from sensation to the world of ideas; "according to imagination," because that faculty provides matter for the operation of reason. The fourth is in reason, and according to reason. At this step, the mind

APPENDIX. 85

is fixed on the unseen world of spirits, their nature and attributes. It is done "in reason and according to reason," because the imagination is now dropped, and the spiritual element alone is the object of thought. The fifth step is above reason, but not beside reason. It rests immediately in God, inasmuch as He can be known by our reason. To this step belong those truths which we know by reason, but cannot comprehend. . . . The sixth and highest step of contemplation is above reason, and beside reason. Its object is the impenetrable mysteries of God which transcend all reason. . . .

There is something supernatural in all these steps of contemplation: for if a man would raise himself up in contemplation, he must do so through the illumination of grace. No mortal can look upon the mysteries of God unless he be lifted up by God Himself to the vision ; all the more, since sin has wrought a thick veil over the eyes of men, which can only be removed by the action of the grace of God.

Contemplation is also distinguished according to its intensity, into three grades: the first is enlargement, when the vision of the soul is wider and stronger ; the second is elevation, when through the influence of Divine light [inspiration] the soul is carried beyond its natural capability, still without being lifted out of the general conditions of its empirical knowledge. The third is alienation by ecstasy, in which, through the action of Divine grace, the soul is placed in such a position that all thought of present things, all consciousness of empirical knowledge vanishes, and the soul is wholly absorbed in the vision of things Divine. The first grade results from the operation of the soul itself ; the second from the action of human activity and grace [inspiration] combined : the third is solely dependent on Divine grace.

Ecstasy can spring from three causes: from the influence of great devotion, from wonder, and from exultation. But the gift alone comes from the free grace of God, though man can, and should, dispose himself for its reception by virtue and pure-heartedness. As the bride decks herself out for the worthy reception of the bridegroom, so should the soul of man ornament itself for the reception of so high a grace. But all this is a mere preparation ; it can never bring about of itself the ecstatic state. It is for man to spread out the wings of ecstasy, but it is for God to set them in motion. A man, however, can lead himself toward that perfection, so that the entrance into the ecstatic state very greatly depends upon his own will ; but even this dependence is conditioned by the grace of God, which is powerful in those who, in morality of life, have advanced to high perfection.

The ecstasy of the spirit can take place in each stage of contemplation. It oftenest takes place in the two highest stages. And then, without any veils of creatures . . . but in its pure simplicity, the soul gazes upon truth. Into this vision the spirit wholly ascends, and the motions of the lower faculties are quieted. The spirit, as it were, soars above itself, above the memory of external things and the sense of the body, and is wrapt in the contemplation of supernal truth. When, in this rapture, the mind is carried away in the contemplation of Divine things above itself, man becomes forgetful, not only of those things which are outside of himself, but of those things which are within him. He becomes wholly self-forgetting, consciousness of self ceases, the multitude of thoughts exist no longer before the mind, and the discursive powers of the reason are subdued under the might of contemplation. The natural light of reason is absorbed by the higher light of contemplation. . . .

Since man in the state of ecstasy is forgetful of all but the object of contemplation, it follows that this is a condition of the highest rest and contentment. And as the state of rapture depends upon the grace of God, so in the ecstatic, man can advance his love of God, and unite himself with Him ever more and more intimately.

But in these higher regions of the spirit, Satanic deception can easily come in. And, therefore, just as Christ had two witnesses of his transfiguration—Moses and Elias—so should the soul, in those realms of contemplation, be accompanied by a test of truth: Holy Scripture. Richard held in suspicion all truth which was not confirmed by the authority of the Sacred Books.

Such is the outline of the scientific attempt made by Richard of St. Victor's to systematize the facts of the contemplative life. He is far from teaching that the mystic method of gaining knowledge is the *via ordinaria*. He teaches the reverse. It is essentially a supernatural state, the result of free grace, and the earnest practice of the soul in the perfection of a moral life. Thus he escaped the error of confusing the two orders, and the accusation which has with justice been brought against Scotus Erigena, of tending, at least in a dangerous way, to pantheistical idealism. As long as discursive methods of the reason, by premise and conclusion, are held as the *via ordinaria* to the knowledge of God, and the mystic method of vision is looked upon as extraordinary and purely supernatural, there will be no danger of falling into the extremes which, for want of a positive theology, the mystics of heathendom and heresy seem never to have been able to escape. . . . [Simply whether the effort is made from the standpoint of the personal ego or the impersonal ego.]

The difference between the doctrine of Erigena and St. Bernard is this: that the system of the former tends to annihilate the individuality of the creature, whereas the system of the latter, though he makes this union as intimate as is possible, asserts the individuality of the creature in its most perfect unity with God. . . .

The work of St. Bernard, Hugh, and Richard of St. Victor's, for this portion of Church-science, may be considered fundamental. What the saint and the theologian began—the saint through the experiences of his own spotless soul, the theologian through holy meditation and the application of science—that Richard's powerful fantasy, clear, logical head, and holy reverence, which kept him steady in the dizzy heights, completed. The Fathers of the Church had emancipated pure scientific speculation out of the hands of the heathen, and our scholastics had perfected their work; but on the science of contemplation—contemplation which has resulted in such marvellous influences on the world—nothing had ever been done in the same way. . . . So it must be considered that Hugh and Richard of St. Victor's laid the broad foundations of their wondrous science—the science of the saints— upon which succeeding speculators built. In the works of St. Theresa, and, particularly of the standard mystic theologian of the Church, St. John of the Cross the influence of these two great and pure thinkers is evident in every page.

One of the best illustrations of the practical results of this mystic science and practice in the busy life of a great scholar, teacher, and preacher, was perhaps the example of St. Thomas of Aquin; and a brief extract from the testimonies to his characteristics, will be not only interesting but highly suggestive.

FROM THE LIFE OF ST. THOMAS.

No doubt the saint's practice in teaching, and the accuracy he acquired by writing from an early age, were of great assistance to him in developing his powers. Then, he possessed another gift, very valuable in the middle ages—particularly so in the thirteenth century, and more especially useful to a religious man—a changeless calmness and self-possession. [Doubtless the immediate result of his habitual contemplations.] Partly through education—through the vicissitudes of life; greatly by character; partly through cultivation of mind, and principally through grace—he possessed his soul in patience. . . . Corrado de Luessia, who knew him intimately, gave a most interesting testimony on oath to the simplicity and purity of his life. He declared him to be " a man of holy life and honest conversation, peaceful, sober, humble, quiet, devout, contemplative, and chaste; so mortified that he cared not what he ate, or what he put on. Every day he celebrated with great devotion, or heard, one or two masses; and except in times proper for repose, he was ever occupied in reading, writing, praying, or preaching." "I saw him," says Corrado, " leading the above life." To this was joined a great confidence in spiritual illumination. His science, says Raynald, " was not acquired by natural talent, but by the revelation and infusion of the Holy Ghost, for he never sat himself to write without having first prayed and wept. When he was in doubt, he had recourse to prayer, and with tears he returned—instructed and enlightened in his uncertainty." . . .

It was not after the modern fashion that the Saint preached. His power did not proceed from violence of manner, fierce gesture, theatrical display, or artificial warmth. There was nothing of brute oratory about him. The exaggerated and excited method of announcing the Gospel, imported from the continent—and which might suit the market place, but ill-beseems the dignity of the pulpit—was unknown to the great Dominican. Doubtless, he felt that the truth of God is too sublime to admit of much human heat in its expression; that a loud manner does not tend to make proof more cogent; and that the Spirit of the Gospel is gentle, calm, and self-possessed : yet firm, earnest, and commanding. Tucco says that " he preached a Lent at Naples on the one text *Ave Maria, gratia plena, Dominus tecum*," and that " during the whole time he was seen to keep his eyes closed in the pulpit, and his head in such a position as if he were looking into heaven." Yet it does not follow because the eyes were closed, that he did not give full expression to his thoughts. . . . Our saint preached ten years in Naples, as well as in Paris, Rome, Cologne, and other places. The people reverenced his word as if it had come direct from the mouth of Christ.

. . . AS A TEACHER.—The quiet, meek young man—so mortified, so recollected—began to let flow that fountain which had been "filled with the waters of wisdom" during his long and deep meditations. His influence over young men was remarkable. It far surpassed—as will be seen—that of any other master. As no other, he could influence the minds of his disciples with an ardent love of study. They were conscious that his teaching had something about it of another world; and the feeling crept over all, and finally mastered them, that he spake as one "having power." . . . From his youth, he had dedicated himself to wisdom as his spouse. The Bollandists say that this spouse of his drew him to herself in such a manner, that nothing could overcome a mind which, in the possession of one reality, possessed everything. Only one thing he asked for—that was wisdom. Even in conversation, his mind clung to its One only Rest—though speaking to man, his eye was fixed on God.

Rainald, his confessor, knew for certain that the Saint gained everything by prayer. On one occasion, during class, the conversation fell on the great Angelical; Rainald burst into tears, and exclaimed, "Brothers, my master forbade me, during his life, to tell the wonderful things he did: one thing I know of him, that it was not human talent, but *prayer*, that was the secret of his great success. He never discussed, read, wrote, or dictated, without begging with tears for illumination." Tucco says that he thus acquired all he knew. This was his daily prayer: "Grant me, I beseech Thee, O merciful God, ardently to desire, prudently to study, rightly to understand, and perfectly to fulfil that which is pleasing to Thee, to the praise and glory of thy name." . . . He wept for the sins of others as if they had been his own, yet so spotless was his mind that he could hardly bring himself to think that man could sin. No one could look on him in conversation without receiving the grace of a special consolation. To meet his eye and hear his voice, was to warm the heart and elevate the soul. . . .

It is often the custom of good men to moralize on the beauty of peace and gentleness- on the charm of solitude and silence; but they do not often go beyond this; they do not often sink into the depth of the human spirit, and seek to discover the hidden spring which produces the great effect. He alone, who has lived to God and to himself, can fully realize the strength and vigor produced within the soul by prayer, silence, solitude; by dwelling under One eye alone, and communing with One only Spirit, and by opening out the whole man—the entire being—like a flower to the sun—toward the warmth and light that is produced by heaven. Great souls, souls made of fine and noble elements, have it in them; it is in their nature, when alone, to seek him who is above, and to find their freedom and their companionship with the world that is unseen. Open the life of any saint; speak to any man who has really given himself to God. Ask him of his silent, solitary hours—whence come all his sweetness and his spiritual light—and he will have but one answer to give. It comes from basking and living in the sun, and by letting the spirit expand itself and grow, with its own spontaneous rectitude, toward Him who made it; from Whom it originally came; and to Whom finally it will have to go. Ask the gentle, silent Young Aquino, how he spent his time. He spent it drinking in the brightness of heaven, and filling himself with the strength of God.

[A brief glance at the discipline of "the School at Paris," at which St. Thomas was so long the leading instructor, will interest the reader of this sketch of his private life.]

The regulations for students coming to the school at Paris were very stringent. . . . Robert of Sorbonne gave a very interesting instruction (*De Conscientia*) concerning what the student should do to profit by his study. This is a *résumé:*

"The scholar, who would profit by his position, ought to observe six essential rules:

"1. He ought to dedicate one certain hour to one specified piece of reading, as St. Bernard advises in his letter to the 'Brethren of Mont Dieu.'

"2. To fix his attention upon what he is going to read, and not pass on lightly to something else. 'There is the same difference,' says St. Bernard, again, 'between reading and studying, as between a host and a friend—between a salute exchanged in the street and an unalterable affection.'

"3. To extract, each day, one thought, one truth of some sort, and to engrave it in the memory with special care.

"4. To write a *résumé*—for unwritten words are blown away like dust before the wind.

APPENDIX. 91

"5. To join with his companions in the 'disputations,' or in familiar conversations—this practice is even of greater service than reading, because it results in clearing up all doubts and all the obscurities which have been left by reading on the mind.

"6. To pray—for this is, in point of fact, one of the best means of learning. St. Bernard teaches that reading should excite the affections of the soul, and that such influences should be turned to advantage in elevating the heart to God, without on that account interrupting the reading. . . .

"In the acquisition of knowledge, the pleasures of flesh must be abstained from, and creature comforts must not be embraced. There were at Paris two masters, bound together, of whom one had seen much, read much, and remained bent day and night over his books; hardly did he take time to say a single *Pater*. This man had only four disciples. His companion had a worse-furnished library, was less carried away by study, hearing mass every day before going to his lesson; and, nevertheless, his school was full. 'Now, how do you manage?' the first asked him. 'It is simple enough,' the second replied, smiling—'God studies for me; I go to the mass, and when I return, I know by heart all I ought to teach.'

"Meditation is not only becoming in the master: the good student ought to take a walk in the evening on the banks of the Seine, not to play, but to repeat his lesson or to meditate."

THE LAST DAYS OF THE MYSTIC LIFE OF ST. THOMAS.

As he approached the end of his great labors on the "Summa," his spirit, which had from his boyhood been living in the world unseen, became more and more absorbed by heavenly things. His trances and ecstasies became more frequent, his converse with the other world more preternatural, his visions and his gift of prophecy, his absorption and his knowledge of men's thoughts, more astonishing. The Hand of God seems to have been placed upon him with stronger pressure, and that bright transfiguration, which is perfected in heaven through the Beatific Vision, appears to have almost begun on earth. As the fruit in the sunlight, day by day, ripens, growing in fulness and deepening in color, till at length it is ready to drop golden from the bough, so the great Angelical seems to have advanced steadily and gradually to his spiritual perfection, till mature for heaven, he was gathered by a Divine Hand, and garnered into the Everlasting Home.

Indeed, he not only dwelt in the Unseen World, but he absolutely conversed with its inhabitants ; so that what was hidden from the gaze of ordinary mortals became visible to him—what we see, was, as it were, withdrawn from him ; what is veiled from our senses was miraculously opened before his eyes. For instance, at Paris, his sister, who had died, appeared to him in vision, said she was in purgatory, and implored masses for her soul ; the Angelical requested his students to say mass and pray for her. Shortly after she appeared to him in Rome, and said she was in glory. He asked her about himself. She said : " Thou standest well, brother, and will join us speedily ; but a greater glory is prepared for thee than for us. Preserve, however, what thou hast." He asked her after Landulf. She said he was in the penal fire. Again, while praying, according to his custom, in the Church at Naples, B. Romanus, whom he had left at Paris as Master of Theology, stood before him. S. Thomas approached his friend and said : " Welcome here! When did you arrive ?" " I have passed from this life," replied the figure, " and am permitted to appear on your account." Overcome by the apparition for a moment, then collecting himself, the Angelical said : " In the name of God, then, I adjure you to answer me these questions : How do I stand ? and are my works pleasing to God ?" " Thou art in a good state, and thy works do please God," was the reply. " Then what about yourself ?" inquired the Angelical. " I am now in eternal life," answered Romanus, " but I have been in purgatory." "'Tell me," continued St. Thomas. " the answer to the question which we have so frequently discussed, whether the habits which are acquired in this life remain to us in heaven ?" " Brother Thomas," replied Romanus, " I see God, and do not ask me more." " How do you see God ?" rejoined the Saint ; " do you see him immediately, or by means of some similitude ?" The other answered: " As we have heard, so have we seen in the city of the Lord of Hosts!" and then instantly vanished. So habitual had the ecstatic life become to the Angelical, that at last he could scarcely fix his mind on contemplation without being carried away in rapture, without being lifted off the ground entranced. At length he was so absorbed in divine things, that even the " Summa " itself failed to interest him. He finally ceased writing after a marvellous rapture which seized him, and shook his whole frame, while celebrating mass in the Chapel of St. Nicholas, at Naples. After this mass, contrary to his invariable custom, he did not sit down to his desk; nor would he consent to dictate anything; and though engaged on the tractate concerning "Penance," in the Third Part of the "Summa," he put away his pen, and became wholly lost in contemplation. Even Reginald, who knew him so intimately, could not account for this. He said, with amazement, to his master: "My Father, why hast thou cast on one side so great a work, which thou didst begin for the glory of God and the illumination of the world?" All he replied was: "*Non possum.* I cannot write any more." Reginald, fearing lest overwork had affected his master's brain, was continually imploring him to continue writing, but the saint ever made the same reply: "I *cannot*, Reginald, for everything that I have written appears to me as simply rubbish." From this time forth, St. Thomas may be said to have lived, not on earth, but in heaven. Shortly after his great ecstasy he visited his sister, the Countess of San Severino, whom he tenderly loved. Even on the journey he was perfectly carried away, and it was with difficulty that his *socius* could get him to the castle gates. His sister, seeing him approach, hurried out to meet him, but he, being so absorbed, scarcely noticed her. She turned terrified to Reginald, and exclaimed: "How is this, Brother Thomas is altogether tranced, and will scarcely speak a word to me?" Reginald replied: "Ever since the feast of St. Nicholas he has been like this, and from that day forth he has not written a word." Then he began again with great earnestness to beg the Angelical to say why he refused to write, and how he had become thus beside himself. Being pressed with such importunity, St. Thomas at length exclaimed to Reginald: "I adjure thee by the Omnipotent and Living God, by thy holy vows, and by the charity which binds thee now, not to reveal during my lifetime what I am about to say!" And then he added: "All I have written appears to me as so much rubbish compared to what I have seen and what has been revealed to me."

In this sketch of the religious life and experience of St. Thomas we have a striking illustration of the truth of the doctrine set forth in these Lesson Helps, concerning illumination, and the impossibility of obtaining the pure unbiased vision of truth except from the standpoint of the spiritual nature, which holds us to the Divine and Absolute. Until the activity of the personal ego and the bias of external education and traditional authority are entirely laid down, and the desire is to know the absolute truth as it is held in the mind of God, and this is sought in perfect confidence that it will be opened to the soul direct from His Spirit, independent of all mediatorial agencies, we are not in the attitude for complete divine illumination. We may develop and exercise the psychic powers and receive more or less of inspiration from the higher plane of the spiritual and Divine, but so long as the pre-impressions and pre-conceived opinions of the external or traditional standards of authority are allowed to mingle with and interpret the psychometric impressions, perceptions, and the spiritual inspirations, we cannot have the perfect spiritual illumination, nor can the psychic powers become the permanent "gifts of the Spirit." The inspiration or illumination of others may lead us to this attitude, but until the inward revelation is direct to our own souls from the Divine, we have not reached the perfect union with God which alone brings complete illumination and immediate guidance from Him.

We must remember that each soul holds the same relations to God and the world, that is held by any and all other souls, and has therefore the same access and privilege of any and all other souls under these relations; hence no soul has taken its own true attitude until it desires and seeks with perfect confidence to unite and walk consciously with the Father in all things, and thus to interpret all things in the immediate light of the Divine wisdom as revealed direct from the Father, and not to interpret the inward revelation by any external standard of supposed revelation through others. Revelation through other inspired souls can be authority for us only as an aid to our attaining the true attitude for the full and immediate revelation of the Father in our own souls. "Verily, verily, I say unto you, He that believeth in me, the work that I do shall he do also," were the words of the Christ.

The mystic fathers in their science of contemplation recognized three grades of advancement, "according to its intensity," by which the soul was opened more and more to inspiration from the Divine, until complete emancipation and perfect illumination was attained. "The first is enlargement, when the vision of the soul is wider and stronger; the second is elevation, when through the influence of Divine light the soul is carried beyond its natural capability, still without being lifted out of the general conditions of its empirical knowledge. The third is alienation by ecstasy, in which, through the action of Divine grace, the soul is placed in such a position that all thought of present things, all consciousness of empirical knowledge vanishes, and the soul is wholly absorbed in the vision of things Divine."

This is complete emancipation from subjection to that which is external to the soul, and the entire circle of the activities of the personal ego, and the limitations of the sense-consciousness, into the freedom of the impersonal ego and the mastery of the spiritual consciousness under Divine illumination in conscious oneness with the Father. No soul should rest satisfied until this experience is reached, and all advanced experiences of other souls are but examples of our own possibilities, to be recognized as such and thus made to stimulate and encourage us to press forward to a like or greater experience; for, as the Lord Christ said, greater even than he had then reached was possible to his followers.

"The first grade results from the operation of the soul itself [the personal ego in its own activity]; the second from the action of human activity and grace [inspiration] combined; the third is wholly dependent on Divine grace" [full Divine illumination].

Among the saints and mystics of the Christian Church, no better example of a self-consecrated and inspired scholar and teacher can be selected than St. Thomas. He earnestly sought, and unquestionably received, divine inspiration in all his work. But sincerely believing that certain generally accepted doctrines had been divinely revealed as fundamentel truths, the bias of this traditional teaching mingled with his own inspirations and served as the principle of their interpretation. The "Summa," to which he gave the full strength of his inspired genius to make it the cream of his life-work, was to be the perfection of theological science, and to be accepted as such by the Church, which recognized the inspiration and masterful genius of the Saint; yet for all his inspiration, and the life-work of his exalted mentality as a consecrated genius of inspiration and scholarship, when he became fully emancipated from the bias and limitations of externally received standards and ideals, by union with God in the realization of the impersonal ego, he discovered that what he had thus written was "rubbish," and he would not complete it. Had he committed to writing what he then saw of the truth, it would (if accepted) have revolutionized the doctrines and utterly destroyed the ecclesiasticism of the Church. He doubtless saw that the time was not ripe for this, and that more harm than good would have resulted from such disclosure. This condition was seen and foretold by the Master in His parable of the wheat and the tares. "Let both grow together until the harvest: and in the time of the harvest I will say to the reapers, Gather ye together first the tares, and bind them in bundles to burn them: but gather the wheat into my barn." The tares of misconception and false doctrine from the sensuous understanding had so intimately mingled and grown up with the pure wheat of Christ's gospel, that the wheat was not then sufficiently developed and ripened in Christian thought to endure the complete separation.

The harvest time foretold by the Master we believe is, however, now upon us, and the sound of the reapers sent of the Master are heard in the field. The tares of misconception, false doctrine, paralyzing dogma, and blind authority are being separated from the original gospel of spiritual freedom proclaimed by the Christ, and bound in bundles to be burned in the fire of a discriminating and righteous criticism.

Had the mind of St. Thomas been free from the bias of traditional misconceptions and false doctrines, and held only the Christ ideal of man's immediate divine possibilities as a spiritual being and son of God, the Saint, on opening his soul to Divine inspiration by contemplation, would doubtless have reached that final emancipation from the external, in the complete illumination and freedom of the spiritual consciousness, at a much earlier date, and have written what would need no subsequent repudiation.

Had this been true of the Church, and especially of the early fathers who formulated their science of contemplation, they would have taken up and carried forward to perfection the higher life of spiritual freedom and supremacy so divinely inaugurated by the Apostolic Brotherhood under the Master's leading.

It was the mingling of the tares of Jewish and pagan superstition with the truth of the Christ revelation, that prevented this result. The second coming of the Christ ideal, separated from all that hides its perfection and perverts its inspiration, is needed and, indeed, is already dawning upon the world.

St. Thomas and the early fathers were honestly laboring under the huge misconception that the doctrine of a morally ruined and lost race, for which God, in the person of Christ, took on our humanity that He might open up a way of salvation through an expiatory offering which should atone for the sin of the world, when accepted by faith, was a divinely revealed truth. With the bias of this fundamental error held as a revealed and basic truth, each advancing revelation to the soul, of the love and goodness of God through an unfolding inspiration, was necessarily interpreted in the light of this external understanding, and all development of Christian thought, however comprehensive and brilliant, was made to conform thereto.

The early fathers seeing the marvelous power developed by the contemplative life among the Orientals, adopted their practice of "Yoga" and asceticism, and transformed it, under the Christian ideal, as held by them, into their improved "science of contemplation" in monastic seclusion. The difference lay in the differing conceptions held by the Christian fathers and those of the Orientals concerning the nature of God and of the human soul, and of the conditions of its existence and further development after what we call death.

The evocations and invocations of the Orientals were changed into the prayers, masses, and invocation of saints of the Church. The contemplation of Brahma in the innumerable manifestations of power in the world, in the spirit of the elements, air, water, fire, etc., each of which was specifically invoked by the Orientals, was changed to the contemplation of God in the one manifestation in Christ as the Saviour of men.

The boundless love and mercy of God was recognized and contemplated in His infinite condescension to take upon Himself our nature and outwork a vicarious atonement in our behalf, without at all perceiving or daring to consider the utter absurdity of the fundamental proposition involved.

Supposing this to be God's own revelation of truth, the contemplation of His infinite condescension in our behalf but opened and intensified the corresponding conception to the mind, of the terrible reality and horror of the fate from which such infinite sacrifice was needed to save us. Hence the lurid pictures of hells and demons, existing to capture and torment forever the souls of men, with which the literature and preaching of the Church have been filled, from the early fathers down to our own time.

Nevertheless, in spite of all this, the mystic fathers and many of the lesser devotees of the Church in all the centuries, did, through the practice of contemplation, attain a marvelous spiritual inspiration and insight, and a high degree of psychic development and corresponding occult power, miracle working, etc.

Their psychic visions, however, were filled with objective representations of their subjective mental states and traditional notions or beliefs. Visions of hells, demons, and distorted caricatures of heavenly scenes, were mingled with better glimpses and purer visions of spiritual and divine realities.

With no proper understanding of the laws and nature of psychic vision, or of the psychic powers and the sphere of their activity, nor of the influence of pre-impressions and pre-judgments upon the partially awakened sixth sense, they were often unable to discriminate between the truth and its distortions in their minds, and thus to interpret correctly their experiences.

The abnormal conditions of mentality, as well as of the nervous system, often induced by their long fasts, extreme austerities, and terrific strain in numerous ways upon outraged nature, awoke visions as monstrous and terrible as those which seem so real to the unfortunate victims of delirium tremens, and none the less abnormal and unreal because the result of religious fervor and the intemperate zeal of a fanatical superstition.

Emancipated from the absurd dogmas and fictitious authority of superstition which so distorted the psychic experiences of many of the earlier mystics, let us turn to the perfect example of the Master, and in its light, perceive and avoid their mistakes, while we recognize and appreciate each step they made in the right direction, and its relation to the splendid results so often reached by them, and be thereby encouraged and strengthened to follow Him in the perfect way.

The early fathers and founders of the monastic system never dreamed of taking the earthly life of Jesus as a literal example to be followed and actually reproduced in its essential features in the practical experience of all men. They regarded Him as a special Divine Incarnation, and therefore another order of being, taking on humanity for a special vicarious work of an official character for man, which he was unable to do for himself, and not as an example and illustration of the higher possibilities of the nature of man brought to fruition in him, and open to all through the following of his example.

This distorted conception of the character of the Christ and of His work for man, and of the salvation He proclaimed to the world, ran through and biased all their thought, teaching, and efforts ; and the pictures it awoke in their minds were projected into their psychic experiences and regarded as spiritual revelation confirming their accepted teaching, the error and absurdity of which broke upon the soul of St. Thomas when he at last came into the clear light of the full spiritual vision.

Had they caught the real message of the Gospel of Jesus in its fulness at the first, that supreme and all-important proclamation of the direct and universal Fatherhood of God, and thus the spiritual nature and transcendent possibilities of man as the child of God, to be realized in experience by the recognition of and loyalty to this Divine nature and relationship, as exemplified in the Master, it would have changed the character of their entire thought, teaching, and efforts at individual salvation.

With this supreme ideal in their practice of contemplation, they would have found early intromission into the light of the spiritual consciousness, and entered into the full realization of the freedom and supremacy of the spiritual life in the flesh. The pagan tares or superstitious notions of vicarious offerings and sacrifices, done away in Christ, would never have crept in to pervert and corrupt the pure Gospel of Jesus with monstrous pictures of hells, devils, and deep damnations of an offended Deity to be saved from. But the recognition of an omnipresent and compassionate heavenly Father whose love, and care, and providence embrace every world and every sphere and every being, and hold them safely in His omnipotent hands, would have filled their souls with the light of hope, courage, faith, and love.

With a true understanding of the salvation promised by the Christ through the following of his example and instruction, the realization of divine sonship, and the supremacy of the spiritual and perfect life in the flesh, a divine incarnation or "the Word made flesh," they would not have so despised the body, but would have cherished and honored it, by making it pure, holy, and perfect, as the divinely appointed instrument of the soul's true work in the world.

APPENDIX.

Though the Lord Christ spent forty days in retirement and fasting during his season of spiritual initiation and complete induction into a condition of perfect and permanent spiritual supremacy, as a preparation for the mighty work of a world's emancipation, upon which he was to enter, he was no ascetic, nor did he institute or command any of the ascetic practices and monastic orders adopted by the mystics of the Christian Church. These were borrowed from heathendom and belong to a condition of life antedating the revelation involved in the perfect ideal and method opened to men by the Christ.

Though again presenting in a living example the perfect life, and teaching, and illustrating the perfect way of life, Jesus did not condemn but commended the consecrated efforts of those who had not the perfect light or method of reaching it. In speaking of the great forerunner who was a thorough recluse and ascetic, and drawing a striking contrast between his life and method with his own, he commended him, saying: "Wisdom is justified of *all* her children." "John the Baptist came neither eating bread nor drinking wine; and ye say he hath a devil. The Son of man is come eating and drinking; and ye say, Behold a gluttonous man, and a wine bibber, a friend of publicans and sinners! But wisdom is justified of all her children" (Lu. vii. 33, 35).

Those who have not yet caught the perfect ideal and method of the Master are not to be condemned for following an imperfect model and way, however erroneous, so long as they are seeking earnestly the highest and best they know. But why should these earnest seekers be left to their imperfect ways when there is a perfect one provided for them? Was not this very missionary work of calling attention to the perfect ideal and certain Way of the Christ, the real commission he gave to his disciples?

This sketch of the method of contemplation practised by the mystic orders of the monastic system, would be incomplete without some well-authenticated facts of experience corroborating what has been said of the working of the system and its results. These we will give from the same authority that furnished the sketch of the method, "The Life and Writings of St. Thomas of Aquin."

A VIVID PICTURE OF THE IDEAL THAT POSSESSED THE MINDS OF THE EARLY MYSTIC FATHERS.

It cannot be too vividly realized that the great doctrines of Christianity broke in upon the world's darkness, as if the night were suddenly lighted up by a flame bursting from the heavens. It is difficult to throw one's self into a state of mind altogether different from that in which we habitually live. Not less astonishment and a less shock was the opening of heaven's gates to the heathen, than would it be were the darkness of midnight suddenly, without any warning, to turn into the brightness of day upon us. He who had been crawling all his life after creeping things and adoring them in his slavish, melancholy, passionate way, is taught to look on the beautiful face of Christ, and to believe. Superstition gives way to genuine belief, and the horrors of an uncertain future, and the insecurity of the present, disappear, as religion teaches man a certain creed with certain prospects, and secures to him a firm and healthy hope in future happiness.

These doctrines wholly transformed the minds of those who received them; their entire moral nature was revolutionized. Men of honest purpose, of deep thought, of generous impulses, shrunk from the moral leprosy around them.

They perceived that the world was steeped in wickedness, and they knew that it would perish. They felt deeply convinced that death is certain, that there is a hell beneath, a heaven above, that sin is to be repented of, that there is a judgment to come, that man has but one soul and that is immortal; and, finally, that the love of Christ is beyond all price, to gain which love is to possess all things, and to forfeit which is to suffer irreparable loss. To love Christ, to save their souls, and to maintain truth [which they supposed this doctrine or these statements to be], these were the master thoughts and motive principles of action in many noble minds during the early struggle.

These men fled from the contamination of the vast luxurious cities into the boundless deserts, to "work out their salvation in fear and trembling." The world might go on and have its fill of wickedness, but they tear themselves away to meditate on death and on the judgment to come, and on the everlasting recompense.

This is a true and vivid picture of the ideal and the motive which possessed the souls of the men who founded the monastic system, and started the practice of contemplation in the early Church. Their attention was wholly diverted from the Christ ideal of salvation in a perfect life here and now, and the corresponding motive of working for the immediate enthronement of the kingdom of God in universal experience on earth, and centered on a personal salvation from the hell, and to the heaven of another world. It is easy, therefore, to see how the strong bias of this powerful impression upon their minds should pervert and distort their psychological and spiritual experiences, which, under the true ideal and motive would have resulted in such harmonious and beautiful realization. The author goes on to say:

These mighty men, these Fathers of the desert, formed a race of themselves. They are the primeval men of the Oriental Christianity, the granite rocks upon which a super-structure might be raised which should endure forever. [Yes, the historic Church was built upon these semi-pagan fathers, rather than on the Apostles. They were the foundation-rock, rather the Christ whom Paul preached.] They seem as full

APPENDIX.

of stability as the pyramids and sphinxes among which they dwelt From youth to old age would they live in the desert, on roots, dates, leaves, or dry bread, and water gushing from the rock. Their life was a continual fast, they slept on the bare ground, they fought with demons, they encountered the hyena and the bear, they wore scarcely any clothing, they continually prayed and toiled, they were stern men, with intensest passion controlled by severest discipline, they were assaulted by terrific temptations, they had iron frames, they lived to a patriarchal age, they were simple, fundamental, and direct in their teaching: to love Christ, to trample on the flesh, to resist the devil, to quench bad thoughts, to pass through life, and to get to heaven—such is the summary of their theology.

Doubtless many of the thoughts they called bad were the pure upspringing intuitions of their spiritual nature, the very voice of God in their souls in protest against their monstrous misconception and perversion of the Christ Gospel; and the supposed insinuations of the devil were often the holy protest of their better nature, outraged by their fanatical abuse of the body's normal functions.

St. Paul (not the Apostle) lived on a few oats and a little water, and fought sleep as he would a tyrant. St. Hilarian, who at fifteen years of age " went naked into the wilderness, though armed with Christ," and whose countenance beamed with a heavenly radiance, lived in a morass, with gnats and flies, amidst reeds and rushes. Peter the Simple became a hermit when sixty-eight. . . . Ammon was twenty-two years in the desert. . . . Anuphrius was seventy years in the wilderness. Spyridion was a shepherd in the isle of Cyprus. Abbot Mark was shut up in a cave thirty years. Didymus dwelt ninety years alone. Abbot John lived three years on a bare rock, without covering, in a mournful solitude. Auxanon, when a child, inhabited a mountain cave. Some passed half a century without seeing a soul. James of Nisibus lived for years in caverns and forests, on roots and leaves, clothed in a goat skin. St. Anxentius dwelt in a wild mountain, and St. Zeno in a tomb. Some lived in fissures in the rock, or on pillars, or in holes in the earth, or in woods and caves, or in the midst of dank marshes, or among the ruins of palaces or of temples of the sun. So powerfully had the influences of the unseen taken hold of men in these terrible times, that what was begun by Paul, and was continued by Anthony, Maccarius, Pachomius, Moses, Arsenius, and others, grew into gigantic proportions.

In more modern times, religious men were called after their founders, *e.g.*, Benedictines, Franciscans, Dominicans, etc. In the first ages they took their names from the place which they inhabited, as the solitaires or monks of Mount Lecthis, Tabenna, Nitria, and Canopus in Egypt. Anchorets lived in private cells. The monks of Mount Cassius, near Antioch, lived in caves; others in tents or cells; the Cenobites lived in common; the Sarabaites, whom St. Jerome calls the pests and banes of the Church, were vagrants, wandering without rule wherever they had a mind. They loved to dwell in cities and castles, and to make a show of piety when they were not overtaken in riotous excesses.

The Stylites, or Pillarists, lived on pillars. Simeon Stylites was the founder of this system. He lived about the time of the council of Chalcedon. He had a disciple named Daniel. The Simeon Stylites Junior dwelt sixty eight years upon a pillar. It is said that Alpius remained seventy years on one, and that two choirs of virgins and one of monks attended him alternately day and night, singing psalms and hymns with him. There were also, though at a later date, religious men in Constantinople, about the middle of the fifth century, who were called " watchers." Their office was to so combine that the divine service should always be going on, something like the " perpetual adoration " of our own day. Studius, a rich Roman noble, joined the order. He built a monastery for the brothers, which was called a Studitæ— probably the first religious institute that took the name of its founder. Lozaman speaks also of the " grazers " who lived on the mountains, never living in houses, or eating bread or meat, or drinking wine. They prayed in hymns and psalms till the time came for their dinner; then each would take out his knife, and search the mountain-side for roots or herbs to make a meal.

Of all the Fathers of the Desert, St. Anthony is the greatest, for he has left a deeper mark upon the world than all the rest. He was the patriarch of solitaires, the keen discerner of spirits, the mighty example after whose pattern the greatest men of the Church have modeled their lives.

The grand simplicity of primeval principles, of foundational example, is exhibited in him. There is but one other more overpowering to the imagination than he, and that is Elias the Thesbite. As others moulded themselves on Anthony, so Anthony formed himself on Elias, and thus brought about an intimate ascetical relationship between the two covenants. [Here is a striking illustration of the fact that the monastic system of ascetic practices was founded, not upon the ideal and method of the Christ and the Apostles, but upon that which ante-dated them, in both Jewish and Pagan religious life, and from which it was wholly borrowed. Anthony sought his ideal and pattern, not in a Christian Apostle or the Master even, but a recluse prophet of a former age, of whom John the forerunner was the latest representative preceding Christ, and of whom the Christ said "No greater prophet has risen among men," "yet I say unto you, he that is least in the kingdom of God is greater than he." And John himself, speaking of the Christ for whose greater work he came to prepare the way, said "I [my method] must decrease, but he must increase." So Anthony, whose ideal pattern and method were pre-Christian, became the model for the Christian saints and mystics that came after him in the mother Church.]

Elias, Anthony, Basil, Benedict, Dominic, Thomas of Aquino, these are the links which connect together, in a harmony which testifies to truth, the heroic teachings of God's purest and noblest servants. The broad principles of St. Anthony's life must be indicated, the grand corner stones must be ointed out, in order that the reader may examine the basis on which the splendid edifice of religious perfection is constructed.

The one living image in Anthony's mind was Christ.

It should be remembered that this image of Christ in the mind of Anthony, was not a man, the Son of God made perfect through voluntary union of will, spirit, and character with the Father, but God himself veiled in humanity, working out a substituted righteousness and propitiatory offering for man as an official salvation, into which he was to enter by sharing with Him in the cross of self-denial and crucifixion of the flesh.

This solitary lays down the monastic principle of St. Benedict. "He exhorted all," says St. Athanasius, "to prefer nothing in the world to the

APPENDIX. 109

love of Christ. His one toil in life was to fit himself for heaven. His great wrestling was with the devils, and with his own thoughts. His marked characteristics were indomitable perseverance and stability in an arduous life. He never looked back, he abode in the wilderness, he fasted rigorously, his bed was the ground, and he strove with hell during a space of nearly ninety years without a single break."

His history is briefly this:—His parents were noble Egyptians of middle Egypt. Like St. Benedict, he despised letters from early youth; like St. Benedict, he, as a child, preferred solitude as his best companion. When he was eighteen his parents died. His ardent, generous mind loved to dwell on the mighty acts of the Bible saints. He knew the Scriptures by heart. He could not get over the thought of the Apostles abandoning all for Christ. Like St. Francis, going into the church one day, he heard the words: "If thou wilt be perfect, go, sell what thou hast, and give to the poor; and come, follow me, and thou shalt have treasure in heaven;" and he was so deeply moved on hearing these other words: "Be not solicitous for to-morrow," that he rid himself at once of all his possessions. He wished to exchange this visible world for the invisible kingdom. He took lessons of perfection from holy men; "he stamped upon his memory their devotion to Christ, and the mutual love which all in common possessed." Satan, perceiving how formidable he was likely to become, buffeted him. But Anthony spurned his impious suggestions, "'setting his thoughts on Christ, and on his own nobility through Christ." This was Anthony's first struggle against the devil; or rather, this mighty deed in him was the Saviour's, who condemned sin in the flesh, that the righteousness of the Lord might be fulfilled in us.

He watched so much, that he often passed whole nights without sleep; and that not once, but often, to the astonishment of men. He ate once a day, after the setting of the sun [a common practice of the Oriental initiates] and sometimes only once in two days, often even in four; his food was bread with salt, his drink nothing but water.
. . . He would mostly lay on the bare ground.

Yet, in spite of his terrific austerities, the spirits of the air attacked him like vultures, and almost destroyed him. He shut himself up in a tomb. A multitude of demons set upon him and smote him till he swooned away under their blows. He was taken for dead and carried out of the tomb. But he slipped back again at midnight, and cried out to the demons: "Here am I. Anthony; I do not fly from your stripes; yea, if you do yet more, nothing shall separate me from the love of Christ." The devils tried another plan; at midnight, while Anthony was in the tomb, he suddenly heard a great crash; the walls of the place seemed to burst asunder, and the foul fiends poured in upon him, changing themselves into the shape of all manner of hideous beasts and loathsome reptiles. [Can any sane mind, unwarped by traditional superstitions, fail to see the similarity of this abnormal experience of Anthony to the deranged nervous and psychic condition of delirium tremens? It matters not the cause of the deranged and perverted activities, whether it is intemperate austerities or intemperate indulgences, the similarity of the result is unmistakable.] The tomb swarmed with fierce lions, savage bears, bulls, snakes, asps, scorpions, and wolves, and all of them, each making its own frightful noise, rushed upon him to destroy him. Though almost speechless from their blows, he cried out to them: "A seal to us and a wall of safety is our faith in the Lord." After this the Lord said to him in a vision: "Since thou hast withstood, and not been worsted, I will be to thee always a succor, and will make thee become famous everywhere."

And Christ poured into him supernatural strength, and he yearned to give himself with still greater abandonment than ever to the service of the crucified.

He was now thirty-five years old. He set off for the wilderness. The devils tried to seduce him, putting the likeness of a silver plate in the way, and dropping bags of gold. But he buried himself in a crevice in a mountain, and here he wrestled and struggled with the fiends of hell, who with yells and clamor and in fearful shapes attacked and molested him. And thus he continued serving God, battling with temptation, for the space of twenty years. [Nothing but a monstrous misconception of the nature of God, of man, and of salvation could suggest that these exercises of a twenty years' seclusion was the serving of God.]

Hundreds now came to him to gather wisdom from his lips. His friends, who had not seen him for many years, marvelled at two things in him: at the vigor of his body—for it "had kept the same habit, and had neither grown fat nor lean from fasting, nor worn by fighting with the demons"—and at "the purity of his soul." And here St. Anthony makes purity identical with self-control and unmoved serenity. . . .

"They wondered again at the purity of his soul because it was neither contracted as if by grief, nor relaxed by pleasure, nor possessed by laughter or by depression ; for he was neither troubled at beholding a crowd, nor overjoyful at being saluted by so many, but was altogether equal, as being governed by reason, and standing on that which is according to nature."

He who lived in the sand, under the burning eye of the sun, amid demons and wild beasts, thus for a hundred years, possessed his soul in patience. It was this mighty force of character, this divine stability, which made him the stem and root of the Tree of Life.

So Anthony groaned daily, considering the mansions in heaven, and setting his longing on them, and looking at the ephemeral life of man. . . . He left his wilderness, and during Maximin's persecution ministered to the confessors in the mines, and to those in prison. . . .

Now he returned to the desert, and increased still more his severity with himself. He put on, and wore till his death, a beast's skin with the hair turned inside. He never washed, and no one ever saw him unclothed till he was dead.

So importunately did the multitude press around him, on account of the startling miracles he worked in Christ's name, that he hurried away from them into the "inner desert," and at length he came to a very high mountain : a stream of clear cold water gushed out of its base ; a few neglected date-palms were the only vegetation which met the eye. He tilled a patch of ground on the other side the mountain ; the wild beasts came and upset his work ; but he forbade them, and they obeyed ; the demons still swarmed about him ; tumults, and sounds of many voices, and crashing of arms, broke through the solitude. At night, the mountain was full of savage monsters, glaring with their eyes, and making the darkness hideous with their bellowing and roaring ; all the hyenas of the wilderness crept out of their burrows at dusk, and surrounded Anthony where he lay, gaping at him with white teeth and red jaws, and threatening to tear his body into atoms. But the cross and the love of Christ were too powerful for the phantoms. This was Anthony's one stay, the image of the crucified in whom he "trusted as Mount Sion." When he uttered the simple words: "I am the servant of Christ," the devils fled away, pursued by his words as by a whip, said St. Athanasius. . . . His energy against heresy caused his fame to spread into distant cities among Greek philosophers, potentates, and priests. He became known as "the man of God." His supernatural power was acknowledged on all sides. His fame spread even to the courts of kings. Constantine, Constantius, and Constans, wrote to him as to a father, asking his advice. . . . It would take too long to speak of his wonder-working power, of his visions, and his prophecies; he saw the soul of Ammon carried up to heaven, he cured Fronto of a grievous disease, he brought health to the Christ-bearing maiden of Laodicea, he cast out devils, and cured numberless sicknesses, in the name of our Lord. . . .

So beautiful and striking was St. Anthony's personal appearance, that men could pick him out of a multitude. "His countenance had great and wonderful grace; and this gift too he had from the Saviour." . . . When over a hundred years old, "he remained uninjured in all his limbs; for his eyes were undimmed and whole, so that he saw well, and not one of his teeth had fallen out, but they only wore down to the gums on account of his age; and he remained sound in hand and foot; and in a word, appeared ruddier and more ready for exertion than all who use various meats, and baths, and different dresses."

St. Anthony was born 251; adopted a solitary life 270; went into the desert 285; supports St. Athanasius 355; died 356; St. Athanasius writes his life 364.

This graphic sketch of but a small portion of the wonderful life of this remarkable man, gives a fair insight into the conditions of that early age when the foundations of the great Catholic Church of Rome were being laid, and of the ideals which possessed the souls of its founders. We can see how the monastic system sprung up as the legitimate fruit of those ideals, and under the consecration and devotion it fostered, we need not wonder at the marvelous experiences both psychic and spiritual that came into their lives, nor at the occult power thus developed and subject to their faith, so generally deemed miraculous. The Easterns had developed and exercised a like power by practically the same processes, but under different ideals. What may we not expect, then, when holding the true ideal of the All-Father and the divine possibilities of the human spirit, we adopt the perfect way of the Christ in seeking conscious union with the Father and the unclouded illumination of the Spirit which this divine union secures?

In spite of the distorted ideals and misdirected efforts of so many of the mystics, Christian and non-Christian, great heights of inspiration and power of service were reached by them. So, with the key of a just discrimination in his hand, the student will find a mine of great spiritual wealth in an unbiased study of the different schools of mystics, and especially of the "lives of the saints" in the Christain Church, Catholic and Protestant.

The key of a just discrimination is a proper understanding of the spiritual nature and constitution of the human soul in its threefold relationship to the cosmos.

The true psychology or science of the soul is yet to be formulated and perfected. The psychology of the schools in the past has been the formulated results of speculations upon the recognized facts of consciousness, and these varying with the cogitations of each independent thinker, no one system has been of universal acceptance. The range of each system has corresponded with the individual conception of the author concerning the true nature, source, and limitation of consciousness.

Most of the psychologists of the past whose authority is recognized in the schools of the present, have supposed sense perception and experience to be the source, foundation, and limitation of all actual intelligence acquired by man in this world; hence, whatever facts of consciousness and experience they found transcending the plane and sphere of the senses, and originating from a supersensuous and transcendental plane and sphere of perception and experience have generally been classed as either hallucination, miraculous interposition—as in the recognized inspiration and prophecy of Scripture—or, in certain perplexing phenomena, as the direct instigation of the "devil."

So strong has been the prejudice thus engendered in the minds of the educated classes, that men of science and letters, for several generations have utterly ignored and refused to recognize or give any attention whatever to the psychic phenomena and facts of transcendental perception and experience, which, though always spontaneously occurring more or less, have been a marked feature of the last two centuries, and especially the last half of the present century. And if during that time any recognized scientist or philosopher accepted the facts and attempted to give them a candid, unbiased study, he was at once ostracized, and cast out of respectable recognition, as a charlatan, etc.

Our own age has the honor of being the first to enlist the attention of the scientific world, and organize societies for the special, careful, and extended study of all psychic phenomena and experience from the standpoint of science, and to institute the deepest possible research into the realms of the supersensuous and transcendental.

Though this work has but fairly begun, the light already thrown upon the psychic nature and transcendental powers of man is revolutionizing the mental philosophy and psychology of the schools, and the newly recognized facts of supersensuous perception and experience are being rapidly gathered up and formulated into the beginnings of a new and all-embracing psychology or science of the soul.

One of the most useful and helpful books on this subject is "The Philosophy of Mysticism, by Baron Du Prel." The author, a profound thinker and philosopher, as well as a thorough scientist and luminous writer, gathers up the well-authenticated facts of transcendental experience involved in dream, somnambulism, and trance, and considers them in the most careful, thorough, and unbiased manner.

Though his conclusions will be startling to many who have never before given the subject-matter serious attention, the suggestions as well as demonstrations offered will be emancipating and extremely helpful to all, and of especial value to the earnest seekers after the higher life.

The author believes that somnambulism furnishes the key to all mystic and transcendental experiences. He demonstrates by it the fact of a transcendental ego in man, holding direct, specific relations with a transcendental world (or, as we should say, with the transcendental or inner side of the one world to which we are externally related through the senses), and having an intelligence and experience entirely independent of and greatly transcending that of the sense ego and sense experience.

No synopsis or brief extracts could give any adequate representation of the ground covered by the comprehensive considerations of this book; so we will not attempt it. The student should take the first opportunity to read and study it for himself. No romance could be more thrillingly interesting to a seeking mind, though it is wholly exoteric in its treatment.

The facts now being gathered up, analyzed, and reported by the British and American Societies for Psychical Research, and other societies for the same work, will play their part in the development of the new psychology. In the meantime there have been many individual investigators and thorough students who have been for years anterior to the now popular Psychical Research Societies, engaged in independent research in this very field, who, through the traditional prejudice, have been ignored by the schools, yet have anticipated results now being popularized by these societies, and indeed greater.

From the standpoint of independent spiritual vision and psychometric perception and analysis, we prophesy that when the work of formulating the new psychology is complete, the threefold nature of man and the corresponding planes of consciousness, relationship, and mental activity, normal and legitimate to him in the body, as outlined in these Lesson-Helps, and adhered to in all our books, will be fully verified and established.

When the sphere of the psychic functions of the sixth sense, and especially the psychometric power, is fully understood, and full discrimination is made between the planes of psychic and spiritual experience, much of the mystery and strange experience involved in the history of mysticism will be readily accounted for.

This practical knowledge of the threefold nature and cosmic relationship of man, and the key of discrimination it puts into our hands, is necessary, to emancipate the world from the blinding influence of traditional misconceptions and false teaching, which for centuries has misdirected the thought and effort of minds seeking light and truth.

No better summary can be given of the fundamental conceptions (or misconceptions) upon which the theological superstructure of Christendom was reared, than that given in the sketch we have quoted from high Catholic authority of the early fathers: "To love Christ, to trample on the flesh, to resist the devil, to quench bad thoughts, to pass through life, and *to get to heaven* [in another world]—such is the summary of their theology."

The entire thought and teaching of the Christian Church from the second century to our own time, in all its branches—Catholic, Greek, and Protestant—has been biased and permeated by these ideals of the early fathers, save in the minds of a very small and comparatively uninfluential minority. To deny the verity of these doctrines in some of the centuries was to evoke the tortures of the inquisition or martyrdom at the stake, under Protestant as well as Catholic *régime*.

"S. Anthony," says our author, "the patriarch of solitaires, the keen discerner of spirits, was the mighty example, after whose pattern the greatest men of the Church have modeled their lives;" and the same authority assures us that "Anthony groaned daily, considering the mansions in heaven, and setting his longing on them, and looking at the ephemeral life of man." And again: "He who lived in the sand, under the burning eye of the sun, amidst demons and wild beasts, thus for a hundred years, possessed his soul in patience." Here was the definite theme of the solitary meditations and contemplations of Anthony, and the basis of his prayers. The mansions of heaven in another world for which he longed, the ephemeral and transitory character of the life on earth which he despised, and which he regarded only as a probationary state in which to prepare for an eternity of blessednesss or misery (the probation ending at death), and the fitting of his soul for heaven by resisting the devil in all the activities of the world and the flesh, which were looked upon as the special field of satanic deception and temptation, these were the ideals that shaped his life and directed his efforts. "His great toil in life was to fit himself for heaven."

Possessed with this idea, it is no wonder that these "men of honest purpose, of deep thought, of generous impulses, shrank from the moral leprosy around them," and "fled from the contamination of the vast luxurious cities, into the boundless deserts to 'work out their salvation in fear and trembling.' The world might go on and have its fill of wickedness, but they tear themselves away to meditate on death, and on the judgment to come, and on the everlasting recompense."

Is it not time for earnest souls to awake from this nightmare of superstition and go behind and above these semi-pagan fathers to the original gospel of the Son of God and Brother of men? He said but little of the world to come, and bade his followers take no anxious thought for the future, as the future would take thought for the things of itself; "sufficient unto the day is the evil thereof." The ideal he held up, for which men were to labor and to pray, was the realization of the kingdom of God in human life and society on earth. "Thy kingdom come, Thy will be done in earth as it is in heaven." He came not to destroy the law and the prophets, but to bring them to fulfilment in the universal experience of life on earth.

The prophetic picture that gladdened the anointed vision of the ancient seers was a redeemed and glorified humanity on earth : " For the earth shall be filled with the knowledge of the glory of the LORD, as the waters cover the sea ; " " And in this mountain shall the LORD of hosts make unto all people a feast of fat things, a feast of wine on the lees, of fat things full of marrow, of wine on the lees well refined. He will destroy in this mountain the face of the covering cast over all people, and the vail that is spread over all nations [the " vail " of sense]. He will swallow up death in victory ; and the Lord God will wipe away tears from off all faces ; and the rebuke of his people shall he take away from off all the earth: for the LORD hath spoken it; " " The wilderness and the solitary place shall be glad for them ; and the desert shall rejoice and blossom as the rose ; " " After those days, saith the LORD, I will put my law in their inward parts, and write it in their hearts ; and will be their God, and they shall be my people. And they shall teach no more every man his neighbor and every man his brother, saying, know the LORD : for they shall all know me from the least of them unto the greatest of them saith the LORD: for I will forgive their iniquity, and I will remember their sin no more."

Here is the clearly defined picture of a perfected and sinless race on earth, foreseen and prophesied of old, to be brought in through the advent and ministry of him that was to come, the mediator of the "New Covenant" relation between God and man, the Covenant of the Divine Fatherhood, sonship and brotherhood, ratified in universal experience.

The mission of the Messiah " which is called Christ," as foretold in prophecy, and the angelic announcement at his advent, was not to save men from the results of sin, as a righteous retribution in the world to come, but to "save his people *from* their *sin;*" save, or bring them to a sinless or perfect life here and now, a life from which no sin should flow. This would of necessity involve the perfect result in all future life, and the only possible provision or preparation for that perfection. This alone will fulfil the Old Testament prophecy of the Messianic work on earth, as well as the promise of the Christ to his followers.

The apocalyptic vision of the beloved disciple on Patmos was this final realization of the Christ work on earth; not the world's destruction, but its redemption and perfection: " And I John saw the Holy City, new Jerusalem, coming down from God out of heaven prepared as a bride adorned for her husband. And I heard a great voice out of heaven saying, Behold, the tabernacle of God is with men, and he will dwell with them, and they shall be his people, and God himself shall be with them, and be their God. And God shall wipe away all tears from their eyes; and there shall be no more death, neither sorrow nor crying, neither shall there be any more pain: for the former things have passed away."

The Church ideal of salvation is certainly not the ideal held up to the world by the Christ and the prophets of all time: yet in spite of the perverted understanding of the fathers, even with their false ideal of salvation, their very retirement from the world, and meditations upon the supreme realities of a spiritual existence, and the contemplation of God in Christ as a Divine sacrifice for man, opened their souls to some most remarkable experiences, both spiritual and psychic. The perverted psychic activities and distorted visions resulted from their false traditional notions and abnormal conditions. What, then, may not be done by a like devotion under the Christ ideal of the universal Fatherhood of God, and the corresponding spiritual nature and divine possibilities of man as the child of God, through the recognition of and loyalty to this nature and relation, when applied under normal conditions?

The doctrine of hell and devils that filled the thoughts of the monastic fathers, and of this world as given wholly over to satanic agencies for the temptation of man, as a probationer for eternity, his eternal destiny for weal or woe unalterably fixed at death, is a heathenish, libelous, and blasphemous caricature of the kingdom and government of the All-Father proclaimed by the Christ, whose infinite, changeless, and omnipresent love and providence embrace all the beings and the worlds of His creation.

This world is God's world, and all things therein have the impress of His infinite skill and holy touch; they are His handiwork and are perfect in the ends and uses for which they were made and to which they are ordained in the infinite wisdom and beneficence of His economy and government. Man has therefore but to recognize and put himself in accord with this divine order, to find God tabernacled in his own life, and the world itself transfigured by the recognition and realization of his omnipresence.

The deep convictions of the early fathers, of the stern and awful realties of the eternal world to which they were hastening, and the pictures of heaven and hell, both of which were made vivid to their minds by constant contemplation of them, stirred their souls to their profoundest depths. This it was which prompted to such self-denying devotion the work of personal salvation.

The motives and the results were none the less powerful for being based on error. It was the consecrated earnestness and fidelity to their convictions that secured the results that were reached, and which would have been unutterably grand and beautiful but for the abnormal conditions and perverted activities engendered by the bias of their misconceptions and false ideals.

These men were familiar with the dreamy speculations of the Oriental world concerning a future existence, involving metempsychosis, reincarnation, karma, etc., with their uncertain and indefinite periods of changing states of existence; hence, with their acceptance of the definite creed which at that time had thus been formulated in the minds of the Christians, they had that sense of certainty of the future life, with its fixed and unalterable heaven and hell, which was sufficient to focalize them in that marvelous concentration of life-effort for personal salvation in another world.

Says our Catholic author: " Superstition gives way to genuine belief, and the horrors of an uncertain future and the insecurity of the present disappear as religion teaches man a certain creed with certain prospects, and secures to him a firm and healthy hope in future happiness."

There is in this suggestion a deeply significant lesson for us. If we reject this monstrous and barbarous creed of the fathers, what shall we put in its place sufficiently impressive to stir us to a like noble and consecrated endeavor? Do we grasp the Christ doctrine of our divine sonship and transcendent possibilities, as incarnate spiritual beings, with sufficient intensity of conviction to make its immediate realization in our own and universal experience the concentrated and supreme motive and effort of our life?

If, then, we accept this ideal, and its realization a possibility here and now, let us, as did the fathers, make our ideal the uppermost and constant theme of thought, meditation, prayer, and contemplation, until it becomes, as did theirs, the burning passion, motive, and inspiration of our souls. Then with the conscious love of the All-Father, and the ministry and companionship of angels to help, in the place of satanic phantoms, or "monsters upon the threshold," to fight us, we shall find ourselves without struggle, effort, or fighting, in the realization.

In the love and providence of the Father, this is the truth of our being. We have only to awaken to its realization. Making it the constant theme of our thought, meditation, prayer, and contemplation is but the process of awakening to its reality.

Throw away at once and forever all thought of rewards and penalties in this world or any other, as a motive of effort, and make the thought of education, not probation, the basis. Let the desire for truth and identification with the eternal realities of life for their own sake be the motive of action, and *your own* will come to you.

The three planes of consciousness and corresponding specific mental action defined in these pages are normal and legitimate to man while in the body, and by the steps indicated may be brought to experience in all who will give the requisite time and attention for its realization.

On the sense plane, man becomes individualized, and learns the value of his individuality in his active relations to other individualities and things; but while conscious of this plane and sphere of relations only, in the struggle for existence and the maintenance of his individuality, he necessarily becomes selfish and self-seeking. Seeing but the externals of men and things he is also easily deceived and misled by appearances.

On the psychic plane, when fully opened to self-consciousness, he comes into direct communication with the inner life and soul of things, and when unbiased by sense standards, preconceived opinions, and self-interest, perceives the truth, or the actual states and relations of all things to which the attention is directed.

On the spiritual plane he awakens to the realization of absolute being and supremacy, in oneness with God and the spirit of things in which all personal considerations and all external and partial standards of judgment disappear. The realization of truth and righteousness and identification therewith make normal and spontaneous the impersonal and impartial attitude of the soul toward all things and all relations on both the psychic and sense planes. Hence the supreme importance of the soul's emancipation from the limitations of self and sense, through the opening of the spiritual consciousness; not for its salvation in a future world, *per se*, but for its salvation to the integral, full-rounded, and perfect life in this world, as enjoined, promised, and exemplified by the Christ.

Says Jacob Boehme : The soul which in this body has entered into the new birth and penetrated to God through the doors of the depth, has great wisdom and knowledge, even as regards the heavens ; for she has come from the womb of the virgin, wherein have been unfolded the eternal miracles of God, and the splendor of the Holy Trinity [the threefold Macrocosm] shines out of her. . . . Dear soul, if you desire the light of God, and also the light of this world ; if you desire to feed your body and to seek for the mysteries of God, do as God himself does. One of the eyes of your soul looks into eternity, the other one into nature. The latter goes on continually seeking in desiring and creating one mirror after another. Let that be so. It must be so, for God wills it. But the eye for eternity must not be turned (away from God) into desire ; but by means of that eye you should seek to turn the other one toward you, and not let it turn away from you, *i.e.*, not let it turn away from the eye that turns into freedom. Put one will into that which you are doing, thinking that you are a servant in the vineyard of God ; that is, into the Eternal. Link your will every hour into humility before God ; then will your image walk in humility with your will in the majesty of God, and be illumined perpetually by the triumphant light of God. . . .

If you rule merely externally (by external means) over all creatures, you are then with your will in an animal quality, and your rule is of an external kind, dealing only with forms. Your desire will then be carried into the animal essence, which will infect and capture you, and you will receive animal qualities. But if you leave that which merely relates to forms [look psychometrically], you will become superior to it, and able to rule over all creatures within the foundation wherefrom they have been created [from the Spiritual].

If you allow nothing [personal] to enter your desire, you will then be free from all things and possess power over all. You have then nothing within your receptivity, and are as nothing to all things, and all things will be nothing to you, in the same sense as God rules over all things and sees them all; but there is nothing that comprehends Him. . . .

"Learn to know the guide from the inner world [intuition] and also the guide from the outer world [sense-perception], so that ye may know the magic school of both worlds. Then will your mind be free from delusions, for in delusion there is no perfection. The spirit must be capable of grasping the mystery. The Spirit of God must be the guide in man's desire Without that man will be merely in the external mystery, in the external heaven of the constellation, which also frequently kindles and drives the human soul; but he has not the divine *magic* schooling, such as exists only in a simple and childlike mind. The external guide works and shines merely in the mirror; but the inner one lights up the essential being. and this it could not do unless guided by the Spirit of God. Therefore, he who knows the celestial school is with God, and will be a *Magus*, without doing much effort, if he is held by God and driven on by the Holy Spirit. . . .

He who hopes to perform something perfect and good, wherein he may rejoice eternally and enjoy it, let him come out of his egoism and self will and enter into submission within the will of God. Even if the terrestrial desire for selfhood clings to him in his flesh and blood, if only the soul will is not infected by that desire for self, then will that self not be able to produce anything, for the will of the soul, resting in submission to God, continually destroys the self-assertion.

. . . Above all examine yourself for what purpose you desire to know the mysteries of God, and whether you are prepared to employ that which will be received for the glorification of God and the benefit of your neighbor. Are you ready to die entirely to your own selfish and earthly will, and do you earnestly desire to become one with the Spirit? He who has no such high purposes, and merely seeks for knowledge for the gratification of self, or that he may be looked upon as something great by the world, is not fit to receive such knowledge. . . . Many of the saints that were driven on by the Spirit of God went afterward from that state of submission again into selfishness—namely, to their own reasoning and self-will. . . . No man can make himself a child of God, but he must throw himself

APPENDIX. 127

entirely into a state of complete obedience to God. Then will God make him His child. . . .

The living soul, from the eternal will of the Father, was breathed into man, and this will has no other purpose than to give birth to His only Son. Of this will God the Father infused into man, and this is the eternal soul of man. The soul ought to put her regenerated will into the eternal will of the Father, in the heart of God. Then will she receive the power of the heart of God and also His holy eternal light, wherein arises the Paradise and the celestial kingdom and eternal joy.

If the soul sinks her will into the meekness, *i.e.*, the obedience of God, she becomes a fountain of the heart of God, and receives divine power, and all her essences become angelic and joyful. Then her harsh essences will also be useful to her, and appear to her more mild and useful than if they had already originally been entirely sweet and mild. . . .

The light and the power of the light is a desire, and wants to come in possession of the noble image made after God's likeness, because it has been created for the world of light. Likewise the dark world . . . desires the same, for man has all the worlds within himself, and there is a great battle taking place in man. That principle with which he identifies himself in his desire and his will will rule him. . . . As the soul is essential, and her very substance is a desire, it is clear that she is in two kinds of *Fiat*. The first is her own soul-property; the other belongs to the second principle, issuing from the will of God in the soul. The soul desiring God, for the purpose of forming herself in His image and likeness, this desire of God acts as a *Fiat* in her own centre; for the desire of God wants to possess the soul. On the other hand, she herself desires to possess the centre in the power of the fire, wherein the life of the soul originates.

The will of the soul is free, and she can either sink into nothing within herself and conceive of herself as the nothing [a derived and dependent being], when she will sprout like a branch out of the tree of divine life and eat of the love of God; or she may in her own self-will rise up in the fire and desire to become a separate tree. . . .

Spiritual regeneration does not depend on learning and scientific knowledge; but there must be an intense and powerful earnest, a great hunger and thirst for the Spirit of Christ. Mere science is not faith;

the latter is the intense hunger and thirst for that which I desire, so that it becomes formed into an image within me, and by grasping it in my imagination it becomes my own property. . . .

By means of the introduction of the Divine will man becomes reunited to God and reborn in his emotional nature. He then begins to die relatively to the selfishness of the false desire and to be regenerated in new power. There is then still attracted to him the carnal quality, but in the spirit he walks with God, and thus there is born within the earthly man of flesh a new spiritual man with divine perceptions and with a divine will, killing day by day the lusts of the flesh, and by divine power rendering the world—*i.e.*, the external life—heavenly and causing heaven—*i.e.*, the inner spiritual world—to become visible in the external world, so that God becomes man and man God, until finally the tree reaches its perfection. . . .

Spiritual knowledge cannot be communicated from one intellect to another, but must be sought for in the Spirit of God. Truly theosophical writings will, even to the intellect, convey here and there a ray of recognition; but if the reader is found worthy by God to have the divine light kindled within his own soul then will the inexpressible words of God be heard by him. . . .

As God is Lord over all, so man in the power of God was to be a lord over this world. The soul in the power of God penetrates through all things, and is powerful over all, as God himself, for she lives in the power of his heart. . . . The understanding is born of God. It is not the product of the schools in which human science is taught. I do not treat intellectual learning with contempt, and if I had obtained a more elaborate education, it would surely have been an advantage to me while my mind received the divine gift; but it pleased God to turn the wisdom of this world into foolishness, and to give His strength to the weak, so that all may bow down before Him. . . .

I might sometimes perhaps write more elegantly, and in a better style, but the fire burning within me is driving me on. My hand and my pen must then seek to follow the thoughts as well as they can. The inspiration comes like a shower of rain. That which I catch I have. If it were possible to grasp and describe all that I perceive, then would my writings be more explicit. . . . I say it before God . . . that I in my human self do not know what I am to write; but whenever I am writing the Spirit dictates to me what to write, and shows me all in such a wonderful clearness, that I often do not know whether or not I am with my consciousness in this world.

The more I seek the more I find, and I am continually penetrating deeper; so that it often seems to me as if my sinful person were too low and too unworthy for the reception of knowledge of such high and exalted mysteries; but in such moments the Spirit unfolds His banner and says to me, 'Behold! in this shalt thou live eternally and be crowned therewith. Why art thou terrified?' . . .

As long as God watches over me with His protecting hand, I understand that which I have written; but whenever He becomes hidden before me, I then no longer recognize my own work, and this proves to me the impossibility of penetrating into the mysteries of God unless by the aid of His Spirit. . . .

These writings transcend the horizon of intellectual reasoning, and their interior meaning cannot be grasped by speculation and argumentation, but it requires the mind to be in a Godlike state and illumined by the Spirit of Truth. . . .

Thus now I have written, not from the instruction or knowledge received from men, not from the learning or reading of books; but I have written out of my own books which was opened in me, being the noble similitude of God, the book of the noble and precious image was bestowed upon me to read; and therein I have studied as a child in the house of its mother, which beholdeth what the father doeth, and in his childlike play doth imitate the father; I have no need of any other book.

My book hath only three leaves [the three planes of consciousness]; the same are the three principles of eternity, wherein I can find all whatsoever Moses and the prophets, Christ and His apostles, have taught and spoken; I can find therein the foundation of the world and all mysteries; yet not I, but the Spirit of God doth it, according to the measure, as He pleaseth. . . . For God bringeth not a new or strange spirit into us, but He openeth with His Spirit our spirit, namely, the mystery of God's wisdom, which lieth in every man according to measure, manner, and condition of his internal hidden constellation; for Christ said, *My Father worketh and I also work*. Now, the Father worketh in the essence of the soul's property, and the Son in the essence of God's own image; that is, in the divine similitude or harmony. . . .

Seeing, then, the Father's property or wisdom is unmeasurable and infinite, and that He being the wisdom itself, worketh, and yet through His wisdom all things do arise ; thereupon the souls of men are diversely constellated ; indeed, they arise and originally proceed out of one only essence, yet the operation is diverse and manifold, all according to God's wisdom. Now, the spirit of Christ openeth the property of every soul, so that each speaketh from its own property of the wonders in the wisdom of God.

For the spirit of God maketh no new thing in man, or it infuseth no strange spirit into him ; but he speaketh of the wonders in the wisdom of God through man, and that not from the eternal constellation only, but likewise from the external constellation ; that is, through the spirit of the external world. He openeth in man the internal constellation of the soul, that he must prophesy and foretell what the external heaven worketh and produceth. . . .

Now, if man (being God's image, in whom the divine speaking, according to the divine science, is manifest) will search the creatures—animals, vegetables, or metals – he must then again obtain grace from God, that the divine light may shine in his science, whereby he may be able to go through the natural light, and then *all things* will be opened and revealed to his understanding. For reason is nothing else but *an human constellation*, which is a dark draught, or resemblance of *all the principles;* it standeth only in an imaginary figure, and not in the divine science.

But if the divine light be manifest, and shineth therein, then the divine word beginneth to speak therein out of the eternal knowledge ; and then reason is a true mansion or receptacle of divine knowledge and revelation ; and even then it may be rightly and truly used, but being void of this, it is no more than an *astrum* of the visible world.

Man is the offspring of God, a spiritual being incarnate or embodied in a physical organism. That part of his being which is pure spirit is necessarily of the essence and nature of the Father's Being, and partakes of the properties and attributes of the Father's Spirit. The divinest conception ever formulated to the enlightened soul of man is the conception of God as

Wisdom, Goodness, and Power, Infinite, Eternal, Absolute.

As the properties of Spirit are all-knowing, all-loving, all-producing, these properties inhere in the spiritual nature of man.

Now, as the object of embodiment is the differentiation of the human spirit from the universal Spirit in an individual personal identity, for the individualization of the self-conscious personality as a child of God, it is necessary that it should first awake to self-consciousness as an individual holding specific relations to other individualities, in a world made up of individual things and relations, under the limitations of a physical organism and material conditions.

While self-conscious only of sense-relations to a world external to man, all his perceptions and experiences partake of the limitations which these relations, under material conditions, involve, in which for the time he is unmindful of his original possessions as a spirit. Nevertheless all these tend to intensify and establish his individual identity as an organic, self-conscious, indestructible personality and child of God.

All the knowledge he can attain through observation and experience under sense-relations is of value to him only as a sense-being, and for its individualizing influence on his personality and the faculties of his soul. They give nothing to him as a spiritual being. His highest possible attainment under sense-relations to the world count for nothing in the wisdom and treasures of the spirit. "The wisdom of man is foolishness with God."

But when fully individualized and established in his

self-conscious personality in relation to other personalities and things, he is ready to be awakened to the self-consciousness of his spiritual nature, and enter into his original inheritance as a spiritual being and child of God. Through individualization in embodiment, he holds the sense of dependence upon, and thus the necessity of unity of will with the Father, that in his personal relations to that which is external to himself he may stand in the wisdom, goodness, and power of God, as His child.

Standing consciously in the inherited (not acquired) possession of the wisdom, goodness, and power of God, the pomp and glamour of all earthly attainment and possession become the veriest tinsel and vanity. Nevertheless, in the light of the higher wisdom, the world and all things therein, external and internal, are seen in their true light, and their divine significance fully understood and appreciated. This is divine illumination.

It was the light of this illumination that Boehme shared to a high degree, and which made him what he was, a God-taught philosopher, and, as he called himself, a "Christian Theosopher," though he knew little from books, or the teaching of the schools. It was this in its perfection that made the unlettered carpenter of Nazareth the perfect man and Christ of God.

Before parting with the illuminated "Christian Theosopher," Boehme, let us quote a few of his words on the necessity of temperance and self-denial on the physical plane:

> The will if it goes straight forward, is faith, and as such it can give the body another shape, according to the external spirit; for the inner

is the lord of the outer one ; the latter has to obey the former, and the inner one can put the outer one into another figure. . . . He who wants to become a master over himself and a celestial citizen must not be a great sleeper, nor fill his abdomen with an abundance of food or drink, whereupon the elements of the devil begin to qualify ; but he must be temperate, sober, and wakeful, like a warrior before the enemy, for the wrath is continually against him, and he has enough to do to defend himself without creating artificial obstacles.

Overeating and intoxication cause sin, because the pure will which emanates from the fire-principle becomes imprisoned and drowned in desire, so that it is rendered impotent in battle. . . . It is the greatest folly for man to crave for things which are not his own, and to introduce into his desire that which infects him with disease, and which ultimately drives away from God, excluding him in body and soul from his celestial state. . . .

Let every Brahman with fixed attention consider all nature, both visible and invisible, as existing in the Divine Spirit ; for when he contemplates the boundless universe in the Divine Spirit he cannot give his heart to iniquity. . . . God lives also in man. Therefore, if we are but seeking and loving our own true self, we then love God. That which we do to each other we are doing to God. He who seeks and finds his brother and sister has sought and found God. We are in Him all one body with many members, each of which has its own functions. . . . We are all one body in Christ, and have all the Spirit of Christ within our reach. If, then, we enter into the Christ, we may see and know everything by the power of His Spirit. . . .

The Godless seek for God outside of his own self, and the Christless sectarians seek for a personal Christ in history ; but the man of God and the true Christian know God and Christ within their own soul. We surely believe in a personal and historical Christ, but only after Christ has become personal in a man will he realize the true nature and vocation of Jesus the son of Jehovah. . . . If you wish to hear the Holy Ghost speak out of the mouth of another you must first enter yourself with your will into the spirit of holiness.

TESTIMONY OF WILLIAM LAW.

From "THE SPIRIT OF PRAYER; OR, THE SOUL RISING OUT OF THE VANITY OF TIME INTO THE RICHES OF ETERNITY."

A few strong words from this inspired mystic of a later date, and in a sense a disciple of Jacob Boehme, will, we believe, prove a stimulus and help to every earnest seeker and student of the higher life of illumination and power. First, treating on some matters preparatory to the Spirit of Prayer :

> The greatest part of mankind, nay, of Christians, may be said to be asleep; and that particular way of life which takes up each man's mind, thoughts, and affections may very well be called his particular dream. This degree of vanity is equally visible in every form and order of life. The learned and ignorant, the rich and the poor, are all in the same state of slumber ; only passing away a short life in a different kind of dream. . . . A life devoted to the interests and enjoyments of this world, spent and wasted in the slavery of earthly desires, may be truly called a dream. . . .
> Do but suppose a man to know himself ; that he comes into this world on no other errand but to rise out of the vanity of time into the riches of eternity ; do but suppose him to govern his inward thoughts and outward actions by this view of himself, and then to him every day has lost all its evil ; prosperity and adversity have no difference, because he receives and uses them both in the same spirit ; life and death are equally welcome, because equally parts of his way to eternity [the realization of oneness with the Divine life]. For poor and miserable as this life is [the life of sense], we have all of us free access to all that is great and good and happy, and carry within ourselves the *key* to all the treasures that heaven has to bestow upon us. We starve in the midst of plenty, groan under infirmities, with the remedy in our own hands ; live and die without knowing and feeling the

one only good, while we have it in our power to know and enjoy it in as great a reality as we know and feel the power of this world over us ; for heaven is as near to our souls as this earth is to our bodies, and we are created to have our conversation in it. God, the only *good* of all intelligent natures, is not an ab ent or distant God, but is more present *in* and *to* our souls than our own bodies ; and we are strangers to heaven and without God in the world for this only reason : because we are void of the Spirit of Prayer, which alone can and never fails to unite us with the *one only good*, and to open heaven and the kingdom of God within us. A root set in the finest soil in the best climate and blessed with all that sun and air can do for it, is not in so sure a way of its growth to perfection as every man may be whose spirit aspires after all that which God is ready and infinitely desirous to give him. For the sun meets not the springing bud that stretches toward him with half that certainty as God, the source of all good, communicates Himself to the soul that longs to partake of Him.

We are all of us by birth the offspring of God, more nearly related to Him than we are to one another ; for " in Him we live and move and have our being.' . . .

God, considered in Himself, is as infinitely separate from all possibility of doing hurt or willing pain to any creature as He is from a possibility of suffering pain or hurt from the hand of man ; and this for the plain reason, because He is in Himself nothing else but the boundless abyss of all that is good and sweet and amiable, and therefore stands in the most contrariety to everything that is not a blessing ; in an external impossibility of willing and intending a moment's pain or hurt to any creature ; for from this unbounded source of goodness and perfection nothing but infinite streams of blessing are perpetually flowing forth upon all nature and creatures, in a more incessant plenty, than rays of light stream from the sun. And as the *sun* has but one nature, and can give forth nothing but the blessings of light, so the Holy God has but *one* nature and intent toward all the creation, which is, to pour forth the riches and sweetness of His Divine perfections upon everything that is capable of them and according to its capacity to receive them.

The goodness of God, breaking forth into a desire to *communicate good*, was the cause and beginning of the creation. Hence it follows, that to all eternity God can have no *thought* or *intent* toward the creature but to *communicate good*, and it is an eternal impossibility that anything can ever come from God, as His *will* and *purpose* toward the creature but *that same love and goodness* which created it. He must always *will* that to it which He *willed* at the creation of it. This is the amiable nature of God. He is *the good*, the unchangeable, overflowing fountain of good, that sends forth nothing but good to all eternity. He is *the Love* itself, the unmixed, unmeasurable Love, doing nothing but from love, giving nothing but gifts of love to everything that He has made ; requiring nothing of all His creatures but the spirit and fruits of that love which brought them into being. Oh, how sweet is this contemplation of the height and depth of the riches of Divine Love! With what attraction must it draw every thoughtful man to return love for love to this overflowing Fountain of boundless Goodness! What charms has that religion which discovers to us our existence in, relation to, and dependence upon, this Ocean of Divine Love !

In what follows reference is had to the working of that " spirit of prayer by which the soul rises out of the vanity of time into the riches of eternity," or awakes from its imprisonment in the life of sense and its limitations, under the law of selfism, to the realization of its spiritual nature and impersonal being as a child of God in the light, freedom, and supremacy of the spiritual life in and over the flesh :

Now, as the flesh hath its life, its lustings, whence all sorts of evil are truly said to be inspired, quickened, and stirred up in us, so the Spirit, being a living principle *within* us, has its *inspiration*, its *breathing*, its *moving*, its *quickening*, from which alone the Divine Life can be born in us.

When this seed *common* to all men is not resisted, grieved, and quenched, but its *inspirations* and *motions* suffered to grow and increase in us, to unite with God, and get power over all the lusts of the flesh, then we are born again—the nature, spirit, and tempers of Jesus Christ are opened in our souls ; the kingdom of God has come and formed within us. On the other hand, when the flesh, or the *natural* man, hath resisted and quenched the Spirit or Seed of life within us, then the works of the flesh—adultery, fornication, murders, lying, hatred,

APPENDIX.

envy, wrath, pride, foolishness, worldly wisdom, carnal prudence, false religion, hypocritical holiness, and serpentine subtlety—have set up their kingdom within us. . . . [These are all the result of the perverted activities of sense life, which would be impossible if the functions of the outward man were under the control of the law of the spiritual life, which is the normal life of man as a child of God. These functions were ordained of God, and held to their true sphere of action work only good. They are as necessary to the highest perfection of life under the law of the Spirit as they are to the animal under the sense law of his life. The body and its senses are the organic instrument and channels of the soul's activities in the performance of its work on earth, and all the fleshy functions in their normal action, are legitimate and necessary to this work; but they can be held to their normal and unperverted activities only by the subordination of the fleshy to the spiritual life. Hence the mortification of the flesh *per se* is a mistaken policy; it will be perfectly regulated and controlled through the recognition of the power of the spiritual life and enthroning it in its rightful supremacy. The great Apostle has given the true method: "This I say then, Walk in the Spirit and ye shall not fulfil the lusts of the flesh." Now the "lusts of the flesh" are but its *perverted* activities, its normal functions being good and holy in themselves.]

This holy Spark of the Divine Nature within man has a natural, strong, and almost infinite tendency, or reaching; after that eternal Light and Spirit of God, from whence it came forth. It came forth from God, it came *out* of God, it *partaketh* of the Divine Nature, and therefore it is always in a state of tendency and return to God. . . . On the other hand, the Divine Spirit, as considered in itself and above, *without* the soul of man, has an *infinite* and *unchangeable* tendency of love and desire toward the soul of man. to unite and communicate its own riches and glories to it, just as the spirit of the *air without* man unites and communicates its riches and virtues to the spirit of the air that is within man. . . . The Gospel is the history [proclamation] of this love of God to man Inwardly he has a *Seed* of the Divine Life given into the birth of his soul, a Seed that has all the *riches* of *eternity* in it, and is always wanting to come to the birth in him, and be alive in God. . . .

Consider the following similitude: A grain of wheat has the *air* and light of this world enclosed or incorporated in it: this is the mystery of its life, this its power of growing. By this it has a strong continual tendency of uniting again with that ocean of light and air from whence it came forth, and so it helps to kindle its own vegetable life.

On the other hand, that great ocean of light and air having its own offspring hidden in the heart of the grain, has a perpetual strong tendency to unite and communicate with it again. From this desire of union on *both sides* the vegetable arises and all the virtues and powers contained in it.

But here let it be well observed, that this desire on both sides cannot have its effect till the *husk* and gross part of the grain falls into a state of dissolution and death; till this begins, the mystery of life hidden in it cannot come forth. The application may be here left to the reader.

I shall only observe, that we may here see the true ground and absolute necessity of that dying to ourselves, and to the world, to which our blessed Lord so constantly calls his followers. An universal self-denial, a perpetual mortification of the lust of the flesh, the lust of the eyes, and the pride of life is not a thing imposed upon us by the *mere will* of God, is not required as a *punishment,* is not an invention of dull and monkish spirits but has its ground in the nature of the thing, and is as absolutely necessary to make way for the new birth as the death of the *husk* and gross part of the grain is necessary to make way for its vegetable life.

It is not the destruction or death of the old man or sensuous nature, *per se*, that the death of the gross part of the wheat grain suggests and symbolizes, but its transformation. The coming forth of the new man is the very process of the transformation of the old into the new. Were the old man first destroyed there would be no objective point in, through, and over which the new could be manifest. It is the germination and bursting forth of the life in the seed, to a new and larger organic evolution and expression in embodiment, which involves the death of the old by its transformation into the new. The very substance of this gross part of the kernel is necessary as a basis for the starting of the new, and is literally converted into the incipient organism of the new. The rootlets reach down into the soil and the blade shoots up to the air and light above the ground. This is the process, not of a dying, but a living transformation of the seed, as the contents of an egg are transformed by the process of incubation into the chick within the shell. Death is but an appearance, a living transformation is the reality. Were the husk and gross portion of the wheat kernel destroyed, there could be no coming forth in organic evolution of the new and higher expression of the life hidden therein. So these bodies, and the powers and functions of the sense life, are not to be despised and outraged, but cherished, and transformed into the beautiful instruments of the spiritual life for which they were prepared and ordained of God. This transformation will come, not by abusing the body, but by the cultivation and coming forth in and through it of the spirit.

> This life of God in the soul, which, for its smallness [of manifestation] at first and capacity for great growth, is by our Lord compared to a grain of mustard seed, may be, and too generally is, suppressed and kept under, either by worldly cares or pleasures, by vain learning, sensuality, or ambition. And all this while, whatever church or profession any man is of, he is a mere *natural* man, *unregenerate, unenlightened* by the Spirit of God, because this seed of heaven is choked and not suffered to grow up in him ; and therefore his *religion* is no more from heaven than his *fine breeding;* his *cares* have no more goodness in them than his *pleasures;* his zeal for this or against that form of religion has only the nature of any other worldly contention in it. . . .
>
> On the other hand, whenever this Seed of heaven is suffered to take root, to get life and breath in the soul, whether it be in man or woman, young or old, there this new-born inward man is justly said to be *inspired, enlightened,* and moved by the Spirit of God, and therefore all that is in him hath the nature, spirit, and tempers of heaven in it. As

this regenerate life grows up in any man, so there grows up a true and real knowledge of the whole mystery of Godliness in himself. . . . He hath then an *unction* from above which teacheth him all things. . . .

But thou wilt perhaps say, How shall I discover this Riches of eternity, this Light, and Spirit, and Wisdom, and Peace of God treasured up within me? Thy *first thought* of repentance, or *desire* of turning to God, is thy *first discovery* of this Light and Spirit of God within thee; it is the voice and language of the *Word* of God within thee, though thou knowest it not. It is the Bruises of thy serpent's head, thy dear *Immanuel* who is beginning to preach *within* thee, that same which he first preached in public, saying, "Repent, for the kingdom of heaven is at hand." When therefore but the smallest instinct or desire of thy heart calleth thee toward God and a newness of life, give it time and leave to speak, and take care thou refuse not Him that speaketh. For it is not an angel from heaven that speaketh to thee, but it is the eternal *speaking Word* of God in thy heart, that Word which at first created thee, is thus beginning to create thee a *second time* unto righteousness, that a new man be formed again in thee in the image and likeness of God. But beware of taking this *desire* of repentance to be the effect of thy own natural *s nse* and *reason*, for in so doing thou losest the *key* of all the heavenly treasures that is in thee, thou shuttest the door against God, turnest away from Him, and thy repentance (if thou hast any) will be only a vain, unprofitable work of thy own hands, that will do thee no more good than a *well* without water. But if thou takest this *unawakened desire* of turning to God to be, as in truth it is, the coming of Christ in thy soul, the *working*, *redeeming* power of the Light and Spirit of the Christ within thee, if thou dost reverence and adhere to it, as such, this *faith will save thee, will make thee who'e.*

Now, all depends upon thy right submission and obedience to this speaking of God in thy soul. Stop, therefore, all self-acting, listen not to the suggestions of thy own reason, run not on in thy own will; but be *retired, silent, passive,* and *humbly attentive* to this new risen *light within thee.* Open thy heart, thine eyes, and ears to all its impressions. Let it enlighten, teach, frighten, torment, judge, and condemn thee as it pleaseth; turn not away from it, hear all it saith, seek for no relief out of it, consult not with flesh and blood, but with a heart full of faith and resignation to God; pray only this prayer, that God's kingdom may come and His will be done in thy soul. Stand faithfully in this state of preparation, thus given up to the Spirit of God, and then the work of thy repentance will be wrought in God, and thou wilt soon find that He that is in thee is much greater than all that is against thee. [This is the essence of the Friends' Doctrine, their specific method of seeking regeneration and the guidance of the "inner light."] . . .

The short is this : the kingdom of *self* is the fall of man, or the great apostacy from the life of God in the soul, and everyone, wherever he be, that liveth unto *self* is still under the fall and great apostacy from God. The Kingdom of Christ is the Spirit and Power of God dwelling and manifesting itself in the birth of a new inward man, and no one is in this kingdom but *so far* as a true birth of the Spirit is brought forth in him. These two kingdoms take in all mankind; he that is not of one is certainly in the other ; dying to one is living to the other.

Hence we may gather these following truths : FIRST—Here is shown the true ground and reason of what was said above, namely, that when the *call* of God to repentance first ariseth in thy soul thou art to be *retired, silent, passive,* and humbly attentive to this new-risen Light within thee, by wholly stopping or disregarding the workings of thy own will, reason, and judgment. It is because all these are false counsellors, . . . they are all born and bred in the kingdom of *self ;* and therefore if a new kingdom is to be set up in thee, if the operation of God is to have any effect in thee, all these natural powers of *self* are to be silenced and suppressed till they have learned obedience and subjection to the Spirit of God. Now, this is not requiring of thee to become a *fool*, or to give up thy claim to sense and reason, but it is the shortest way to have thy sense and reason delivered from folly and thy whole rational nature strengthened, enlightened, and guided by that Light which is Wisdom itself.

A child that obediently denies his own will and reason to be guided by the will and reason of a truly wise and understanding tutor, cannot be said to make himself a fool, and give up the benefit of his own rational nature, but to have taken the shortest way to have his own will and reason made truly a blessing to him. . . .

But thou wilt perhaps say, if *all self-love* is to be renounced, then all love of our neighbor is renounced along with it, because the commandment is only "to love our neighbor as ourselves." The answer here is easy, and yet no quarter given to self-love. There is but *one only* love in heaven, and yet the angels of God love one another in the same manner as they love themselves. The matter is thus: the one supreme, unchangeable rule of love, which is a law of all intelligent beings of all worlds, and will be a law to all eternity, is this, viz., *that God alone is to be loved for Himself, and all other beings only in Him and for Him.* Whatever intelligent creature lives not under this rule of love, is so far fallen from the order of his creation, and is, till he returns to this eternal Law of Love, an *apostate* from God, and incapable of the kingdom of heaven. . . . But what is loving any creature only *in* and *for* God ? It is when we love it only as it is God's *work, image,* and *delight;* when we love it merely as it is God's and belongs to Him ; this is loving it in God. This is the *one love* that is, and must be the spirit of all creatures that live united to God.

But to return and further show how the soul that feels the call of God to repentance is to behave under it, that this stirring of the Divine Power in the soul may have its full effect, and bring forth the birth of the new man in Christ Jesus. We are to consider it (as in truth it is) as the *Seed* of the Divine Nature within us, that can only grow by its *own strength* and *union* with God. It is the Divine Life, and therefore can grow from nothing but Divine Power. . . . Now, this truth is easily consented to, and a man thinks he believes it because he consents to it, or rather does not deny it. But this is not enough ; it is to be apprehended in a deep, full, and practical assurance in such a manner as a man knows and believes that he did not create the stars, or cause life to rise up in himself. And then it is a belief that puts the soul into a right state, that makes room for the operation of God upon it. The light then enters with full power into the soul, and His Holy Spirit moves and directs all that is done in it, and so man lives again in God as a new creature. For this truth, thus firmly believed, will have these two most excellent effects :

First—It will keep the soul fixed and continually turned toward God, in faith, prayer, desire, confidence, and resignation to Him, for all that it wants to have done in it and to it ; which will be a continual source of all divine virtues and graces. The soul thus turned to God must be always receiving from Him. It stands at the true door of all divine communications, and the Light of God as freely enters into it as the light of the sun enters into the *air*.

Second.—It will fix and ground the soul in a true and lasting self-

APPENDIX. 143

denial. For by thus knowing and owning our own *nothingness* and inability that we have no other capacity for good but that of receiving it from God alone, *self* is wholly denied, its kingdom is destroyed, no room is left for spiritual pride and self-esteem ; we are saved from a pharisaical holiness, from wrong opinions of our own works and good deeds, and from a multitude of errors, the most dangerous to our souls, all which arise from the *something* that we take ourselves to be either in nature or grace. But when we once apprehend but in some good degree the *All* of God and the *nothingness* of ourselves, we have got a Truth whose usefulness and benefit no words can express. It brings a kind of infallibility into the soul in which it dwells ; all that is vain, and false, and deceitful is forced to vanish and fly before it. When our religion is founded on this Rock, it has the firmness of a rock and its height reaches unto heaven. The world, the flesh, and the devil can do no hurt to it ; all enemies are known, and all disarmed by this great Truth dwelling in our souls. It is the knowledge of the *All* of God that makes Cherubims and Seraphims to be the flames of Divine Love. For where this *All* of God is truly known and felt in any creature, there its whole breath and spirit is a fire of love ; nothing but a pure, disinterested love can rise up in it, or come from it—a love that begins and ends in God—and where this love is born in any creature, there a seraphic life is born along with it ; for this pure love introduces into the *All* of God—all that is in God is opened in the creature ; it is united with God, and hath the life of God manifest in it.

There is but one *salvation* for all mankind, and that is [the realization of] the *Life of God* in the soul. God has but *one design* or intent toward all mankind, and that is to *introduce* or *generate* His own Life, Light, and Spirit in them, that all may be so many images, temples, and habitations of Himself. This is God's will to all *Christians, Jews,* and *Heathens.* They are all *equally* the desire of His heart ; His light continually *waits* for an entrance into *all* of them ; His "wisdom crieth, she putteth forth her voice," not here, or there, but everywhere, in all the streets of all the parts of the world.

Now, there is but *one possible* way for man to attain this salvation or Life of God in the soul. There is not one for the *Jew,* another for a *Christian,* and a third for the *Heathen.* No ; God is one, human nature is one, salvation is one, and the Way to it is one ; and that is *the desire of the soul turned to God.* When this *desire* is alive and breaks forth in any creature under heaven, then the *lost sheep* is found, and the *Shepherd* hath it upon His shoulders. Through *this desire* the poor *prodigal son* leaveth his *husks* and swine and hasteth to his Father; it is because of *this desire* that the Father seeth the son while yet *afar off*, that he runs out to meet him, falleth on his neck, and kisseth him. See here how plainly we are taught that no sooner is this desire *arisen* and in *motion* toward God, but the *operation* of God's Spirit answers to it, cherishes and welcomes its *first beginnings*, signified by the Father's seeing, and having compassion on His son while yet *afar off*—that is, in the first beginnings of his desire. Thus does *this desire* do all: it brings the soul to God, and God into the soul; it unites with God, it co-operates with God, and is one life with God. Suppose this *desire* not to be alive, not in motion either in a Jew or a Christian, and then all the sacrifices, the service, the worship, either of the Law or the Gospel, are but *dead* works that bring *no life* into the soul, nor beget any *union* between God and it. Suppose this desire to be awakened and fixed upon God, though in souls that never heard either of the Law or the Gospel, and then the Divine Life or operation of God enters into them, and the *new birth in Christ* is formed in those that never heard of His name. And these are they "that shall come from the east, and from the west, and sit down with Abraham and Isaac in the kingdom of God."

O my God, just and good, how great is Thy love and mercy to mankind, that heaven is everywhere open and Christ thus the *common* Saviour to all that turn the desire of their hearts to Thee!

O sweet Power of the Bruiser of the serpent, born in every son of man, that stirs and works in every man and gives every man a power and desire to find his happiness in God! O holy Christ, heavenly "Light, that lighteth every man that cometh into the world," that redeemeth every soul that followeth thy light, which is *always within him*. O Holy Being, immense Ocean of Divine Love, in which all mankind live, and move, and have their being! None are separated from Thee, none live out of Thy love, but all are embraced in the arms of Thy mercy, all are partakers of Thy Divine Life, the operation of Thy Holy Spirit, as soon as their heart is turned to Thee! O plain and easy and simple way of salvation! wanting no subtleties of art or science, no borrowed learning, no refinements of reason, but all done by the simple, natural motion of every heart that truly longs after God. For no sooner is the finite desire of the creature in motion toward God but the infinite desire of God is united with it, co-operates with it. And in this united desire of God and the creature is the salvation of the soul brought forth. For the soul is shut out of God, and imprisoned in its own dark workings of flesh and blood, merely and solely because it desires to live to the vanity of this world. This *desire* is its darkness, its death, its imprisonment, and separation from God.

When, therefore, the *first spark* of a desire after God arises in the soul, cherish it with all thy care, give all thy heart into it; it is nothing less than a touch of the divine Lodestone that is to draw thee out of the vanity of time into the riches of eternity. Get up, therefore, and follow it as gladly as the *wise men of the East* followed the *star* from heaven that appeared to them. It will do for thee as the star did for them; it will lead thee to the birth of the Christ in the dark centre of thine own soul. . . .

But that thou mayest do all this the better, and be more firmly assured that this *resignation* to and *dependence* upon the working of God's Spirit within thee is right and sound, I shall lay before thee two great and infallible and fundamental truths, which will be as a rock for thy faith to stand upon.

First—That through all the whole of things nothing can *do* or *be* a real good to thy soul but the *operation of God* upon it. *Second*—That all the dispensations of God to mankind, from Adam to the preaching of the Gospel, were only for this *one end*—to fit, prepare, and dispose the soul for the *operation* of the Spirit of God upon it. These two great truths, well and deeply apprehended, put the soul in its right state, in a continual source of light, in thy mind.

They will keep thee safe from all errors, and false zeal in things, and forms of religion—from a sectarian spirit, from bigotry and superstition; they will teach thee the true difference between the *means* and the *end* of religion, and the regard thou showest the *shell* will be only so far as the kernel is to be found in it. . . .

All the sacrifices and institutions of the ancient patriarchs, the *Law* of *Moses* with all its types and rites and ceremonies, had this *only end:* they were the methods of Divine Wisdom for a time, to keep the hearts of men from the wanderings of idolatry, in a state of *holy expectation* upon God; they were to keep the *first Seed* of life in a state of growth, and make way for the further operation of God upon the soul; or, as the Apostle speaks, to be a *schoolmaster leading us to Christ.*

APPENDIX.

Man had broke off from his true *centre*, his proper place in God, and therefore the Life and operation of God was no more in him. He was fallen from a life in God into a life of *self*, into an animal life of self-love, self-esteem, and self-seeking in the poor, perishing enjoyments of this world. . . . All sin, death, damnation, and hell is nothing else but this kingdom of *self*, or the various operations of self-love and self-seeking which separate the soul from God. . . .

On the other hand, all that is *grace, redemption, salvation, sanctification, spiritual life*, and the *new birth*, is nothing else but so much of the Life and operation of God found again in the soul. It is man come back again into his *centre* or *place* in God, from whence he had broke off. . . .

This Pearl of eternity is the Church, or temple of God, *within thee*, the consecrated place of divine worship, where alone thou canst worship God "in spirit and in truth." In *spirit*, because thy spirit is that alone in thee which can unite and cleave unto God, and receive the workings of His Divine Spirit upon thee. *In truth*, because this adoration in spirit is that *truth* and *reality* of which all outward *forms* and *rites*, though instituted by God, are only the *figure* for a time ; but this worship is eternal. Accustom thyself to the holy service of this inward temple ; in the midst of it is the Fountain of living water, of which thou mayest drink and live forever. There the mysteries of thy redemption are celebrated or, rather, opened in life and power. . . . When once thou art well grounded in this *inward worship* thou wilt have learnt to live unto God above time and place ; for every day will be Sunday to thee, and wherever thou goest thou wilt have a *priest*, a *church*, and an *altar* along with thee. For when God has all that He should have of thy heart, when, renouncing the will, judgment, tempers, and inclinations of thy old man, thou art wholly given up to the obedience, to the Light, and Spirit of God within thee, to *will* only in His Will, to love only in His Love, to be wise only in His Wisdom ; then it is that everything thou dost is a song of praise, and the common business of thy life is a conforming to God's will on earth as angels do in heaven.

I shall conclude this part with the words of the heavenly illuminated and blessed man, Jacob Boehme : " It is much to be lamented that we are so blindly led, and the truth withheld from us through imaginary conceptions ; for if the Divine Power in the inward ground of the soul

APPENDIX. 147

was manifest and working with its lustre in us, then is the whole Triune God present in the *life* and *will* of the soul, and the heaven wherein God dwelleth is opened in the soul in the *place* where the Father begetteth His Son, and where the Holy Ghost proceedeth from the Father and the Son."

We give but a fragment from the writings of these two great mystics and Illuminati of the Protestant branch of Christendom. Persecuted and exiled from the recognition and fellowship of the popular communion of their own time, yet walking with God in the light and power of the Spirit, their experience and testimony will live to enlighten, strengthen, and encourage generations to come, when their persecutors are buried in oblivion.

The revival of interest on every hand in the higher possibilities of man will lead to the rescue of many of these rich treasures of mystic experience and testimony from the obscurity to which ecclesiastic bigotry and intolerance had consigned them, and the opening of them to the awakening religious thought of our age will be of inestimable service.

The experience and testimony of the early "Friends," the Quietists, and of other orders recognizing the inward light, and representing a high degree of spiritual awakening, though receiving the ban and generally the persecution of the Church of their day, furnish striking illustrations of the power which a living inspiration opens in the life of man. They point also to the time when, emancipated from the trammels of ecclesiastical authority and the limitations of traditional ideals, all shall "come in the unity of the faith, and of the knowledge of the Son of God, unto a perfect man, unto the measure of the stature of the fulness of Christ."

The lives of many of these mystics of the various orders were attended with experiences of the most marvelous character, generally deemed miraculous, and so were regarded as exceptional. Blinded by the bias of traditional misconception, it did not occur to many of them that occult power over material elements and conditions was the legitimate and necessary result of spiritual supremacy in the personal life. Hence, this was not expected only as an exceptional experience through a miraculous interposition, as a special favor of Divine Providence in special emergencies.

The experience as well as the testimony of all these spiritually awakened and enlightened souls, however, combine to confirm the great fundamental truth of the Master's teaching, that the kingdom of God is not something to be sought for as external, but an inward experience. It must be found and realized through the conscious union of the soul with God in the heights and depths of its own spiritual being, and this in *many* souls, before it can be embodied in the organized activities of men as the new and divine social order, in which the will of the All-Father shall be done on earth as it is in heaven.

When George Fox went into Scotland preaching his doctrine of the inner light, he met with great opposition from the clergy, in which they drew up a number of curses to be read in the "steeple-houses," to which all the people were to say Amen. One of these was, "Cursed is he that saith 'Every man hath a light within him sufficient to lead him to salvation,' and let all the people say Amen." Another was, "Cursed is he that saith 'Faith is without sin,' and let all the people say Amen." To these the great apostle of the " inner light " replied :

Concerning the light, Christ saith, Believe in the light, that ye may become children of light ; and he that believeth shall be saved ; he that believeth shall have everlasting life ; he that believeth passeth from death unto life, and is grafted into Christ. 'And ye do well,' saith the Apostle, ' that ye take heed unto the light that shines in a dark place, until the day dawn, and the day-star arise in your hearts. So the light is sufficient to lead unto the day-star.' As concerning faith, it is the gift of God, and every gift of God is pure. The faith which Christ is the author of is precious, divine, and without sin. This is the faith which gives victory over sin and access to God ; in which faith they please God. But those are reprobates themselves concerning this faith, and are in their dead faith, who charge sin upon this faith under pain of a curse, which faith gives victory over their curse, and returns it into their own bowels.

From an address to Friends we take the following :

' Quench not the Spirit, nor despise prophesyings,' when it moves ; neither hinder babes and sucklings from crying Hosanna ; for out of their mouths will God ordain strength. There were some in Christ's day that were against such, whom He reproved ; and there were some in Moses' day who would have stopped the prophets in the camp ; whom Moses reproved, and said by way of encouragement to them, ' Would God that all the Lord's people were prophets.' So I say now to you. Therefore ye that stop it in yourselves, do not quench it in others, neither in babe nor suckling. . . . Let not the sons and daughters, nor the handmaids, be stopped in their prophesyings, nor the young men in their visions, nor the old men in their dreams ; but let the Lord be glorified in and through all, who is over all, God blessed forever ! So everyone may improve their talents, everyone exercise their gifts, and everyone speak as the Spirit gives them utterance. . . . ' For the manifestation of the Spirit is given to everyone to profit withal.'

APPENDIX.

Being finally arrested at the instigation of the priests and brought before the council, he says of the event: When I had stood awhile, and they said nothing to me, I was moved by the Lord to say, Peace be amongst you. Wait in the fear of God, that ye may receive His wisdom from above, by which all things were made and created; that by it ye may all be ordered, and may order all things under your hands to God's glory. They asked me what was the occasion of my coming into that nation? I told them I came to visit the seed of God, which had long lain in bondage under corruption; that all in the nation who professed the Scriptures, the words of Christ, of the prophets and apostles, might come to the light, Spirit, and power which they were in who gave them forth; that in and by the Spirit, they might understand the Scriptures, and know Christ and God aright, have fellowship with them and one with another.

This little fragment from Fox gives a slight hint of his powerful character and teaching. The record of his remarkable life and labors and those of his compeers is accessible to all, and will repay a careful study.

We will close this fragmentary glimpse into the teaching of the mystics with a few excerpts from Cornelius Agrippa and several Neo-Platonists of the earlier centuries. Agrippa was regarded by Thomas Vaughan, from whom we have quoted, as the prince of mystics and adepts or true magi. Agrippa says, as quoted by Franz Hartman:

Those who attempt to solve the problems of the divine secrets of nature by the reading of books will remain in the dark; they are led away from the light of reason by the illusive glare of their erring intellect; they are misguided by the tricks of external astral influences and by erroneous imaginations. They fall continually into error by seeking beyond their ownselves that which exists within themselves.

You must know that the great cause of all magic effects is not external to ourselves, but operating within ourselves, and this cause can produce all that the magicians, astrologers, alchemists, or necromancers ever produced. Within ourselves is the power which produces all wonderful things.

Magic science embraces a knowledge of the most sublime and exalted truths, the deepest mysteries in nature, the knowledge of the nature of matter and energy, of the attributes and qualities of all things. By uniting the powers of nature and combining the lower with its corresponding higher counterpart, the most surprising effects may be produced. This science is therefore the highest and most perfect of all. Agrippa regards nature as being a trinity [a threefold Macrocosm], an elementary (corporeal), astral, and spiritual world, and the lower principles are intimately connected with the higher ones. . . .

The cause of all activity in the universe is the omnipresent principle of Life (being identified with Will), a function of the universal Spirit. This life-principle causes the ethereal Soul to act upon the gross element of Matter.

The Spirit—the *Primum mobile*—is self-existent and in motion ; the body. or the element of matter, is, in its essence, without motion, and differs so much from the former that an intermediary substance is required by which the Spirit can be united with the body. This intermediary spiritual substance is the soul, or the fifth essence (*quinta essentia*), because it is not included in the four states of matter which are called the four elements, but constitutes a fifth element, or a higher state of that matter which is perceptible to the physical senses. This soul of the world is of the same form as the world, because as the spirit in man acts upon all the members of his body by means of man's soul, likewise the universal Spirit, by means of the soul of the universe, pervades and penetrates all parts of the latter. There is nothing in the world which does not contain a spark of this universal power ; but it is most active in those things or beings in whom the activity of soul is strongest. . . .

God created man in His own image. The universe is the image of God, and man is the image of nature. Man is, therefore, so to say, the image of the image ; or in other words, a *Microcosmos* or little world. The world is a reasonable living and immortal being; man is equally reasonable, but he is mortal, or at least divisible. *Hermes Trismegistus* says that the world is immortal, because no part of it is ever annihilated. Nothing is ever annihilated, and if " to die " means to be annihilated, then is " dying " a term without any reason for its existence, because there is no death in nature. If we say that a man dies, we do not mean to imply that anything of that man perishes; we only mean to say that his body and soul become separated from each other. . . . God is infinite and cannot be overpowered by anything, and likewise is man's spirit free and can neither be forced nor limited. In God is contained the whole world and everything existing therein, and likewise in the will of man is contained every part of his body. Man being thus stamped and sealed in the image of God as His counterpart necessarily clothed himself in a form representing the true image of nature. He is, therefore, called the second or little world; he contains everything contained in the great world. and there is nothing contained in the latter which is not also truly existing within the organism of man. . . . Man is, therefore, called by the Bible "the whole creation," and in his aspect as the Microcosm he contains not only all parts of the world, but also contains and comprehends the divinity itself.

The natural soul is the *Medium* by which the Spirit becomes united with the flesh and the body, through which the latter lives and acts and exercises its functions. . . . This is the doctrine of all hermetic philosophers. Man consists of the higher, the intermediary, and the lower principles [spirit, soul, and body]. . . . That part which is called the rational soul, and which, being free. may choose between the higher and the lower, will, if it continually clings to the highest, become united with God and immortal in Him; but if the intellectual principle clings to that which is evil, it will become ultimately evil and grow to be a malicious demon. . . .

It is possible that if the thoughts of the wise are directed with great intensity upon God, the divine light illuminates the mind and radiates its rays through all parts of the dark and gross body, causing even the latter to become illuminated like a luminous star, and to change its attraction to the earth, so that it may be raised up into the air, and thus it has happened that even the physical bodies of men have been carried away to some distant locality. . . . [We read of such an experience with Philip the Apostle, who, after baptizing the Eunuch of Ethiopia, was immediately transported in the power of the Spirit to another town. "And when they were come up out of the water the Spirit of the Lord caught away Philip, that the Eunuch saw him no more: and he went on his way rejoicing. But Philip was found at Azotus; and passing through he preached in all the cities till he came to Cæsarea."]

APPENDIX. 153

Man's power to think increases in proportion as this ethereal and celestial power of light penetrates his mind, and strengthening his mental faculties, it may enable him to see and perceive that which he interiorly thinks, just as if it were objective and external. Spirit being unity and independent of our ideas of space, and all men having therefore essentially the same spirit, the souls of men existing at places widely distant from each other, may thus enter into communication and converse with each other exactly in the same manner as if they had met in their physical bodies. In this state man may perform a great many things in an exceedingly short period of time, so that it may seem to us as if he had required no time at all to perform it. . . . Such a man is able to comprehend and understand everything by the light of the universal power or guiding intelligence with which he is spontaneously united. . . .

The spirit may accomplish a great deal by the power of *Faith*. This power is a firm confidence or conviction, based upon the knowledge that one can and will accomplish his purpose. It is a strong, unwavering attention which gives strength to the work, causing, so to say, an image in our mind of the power which is necessary to accomplish the work, and of the work which is to be accomplished in, by, and through ourselves. We must, therefore, in all magic operations, apply a strong will, a vivid imagination, a confident hope, and a firm faith, all of which combined will assist in producing the desired result. . . .

There is an art, known only to few, by which the purified and faithful soul of man may be instructed and illuminated, so as to be raised at once from the darkness of ignorance to the light of wisdom and knowledge. There is also an art by which the knowledge gained by the impure and unfaithful may be taken away from their mind and memory and they thus be reduced to their former state of ignorance. . . . If the soul is perfectly purified and sanctified she becomes free in her movements, she sees and recognizes the divine light, and she instructs herself, while she seems to be instructed by another. In that state she requires no other admonition except her own thought, which is the head and guide of the soul. She is then no more subject to terrestrial conditions of time, but lives in the eternal, and for her to desire a thing is to possess it already.

C. Agrippa here adds the following instructions, copied from Boethius: "The guides on the road to perfection are Faith, Hope, and Charity, and the means to attain this object are Purity, Temperance, Self-control, Chasity, Tranquillity of Mind, Contemplation, Adoration (Ecstasy), Aspiration, and Virtue.

If the highest state of spiritual development is attained, the spirit, endowed with the highest spiritual activity of the soul, attracts the truth and perceives and knows at once the conditions, causes, and effects of all external and internal, natural and divine, things. It sees them within the external like in a mirror of eternity. By this process, *Man*, while he still remains in external nature, may know all that exists in the internal and external world, and see all things, not merely those which are, but also those which have been or which will exist in the future, and, moreover, by being united and identified with divine power, he obtains the power to change things by the power of his *Word*. Thus man, being within nature, may be above her and control her laws.

Apularius says that the human soul may be put into a state of sleep, so that she will forget her terrestrial conditions, and turning her whole being toward her divine origin, she will become illuminated by the divine light, and not only be able to see the future and to prophesy it correctly, but also to receive certain spiritual powers. On such occasions the divine inspiration and illumination may be so great as even to communicate itself to other persons near, and to influence them in a similar manner. . . .

This is nothing more nor less than the ecstatic or spiritual trance referred to in these Lesson-Helps and our other books, and which is all that this author describes; but it is abnormal, inasmuch as the state is not correlated with the external consciousness, this being closed or put to sleep in the trance. What we want and may have is the same degree of illumination without the closing of external consciousness, but its co-ordination with the spiritual.

Only those who are pure-minded and spiritual can possess true magic powers. Thought is the supreme power in man, and pure spiritual thought is the miracle worker within him. If the thought of man is bound to the flesh, deeply amalgamated with it, and occupied with ani-

APPENDIX. 155

mal desires, it loses power over the divine element, and therefore among those who seek to exercise magical powers there are few who succeed.

Porphyry says: "The Incorporeal governs the Corporeal, and is therefore present everywhere, although not as space, but in power. The corporeal existence of things cannot hinder the incorporeal from being present to such things as it desires to enter into relation with. The soul has, therefore, the power to extend her activity to any locality she may desire. She is a power which has no limits, and each part of her, being independent of special conditions, can be present everywhere, provided she is pure and unadulterated with matter. Things do not act upon each other merely by the contact of their corporeal forms, but also at a distance, provided they have a soul, because the higher elements of the soul are everywhere and cannot be enclosed in a body like an animal in a cage or a liquid in a bottle. The universal soul being essentially one and identical with the infinite Supreme Spirit, may by the infinite power of the latter discover and produce everything, and an individual soul may do the same thing if she is purified and free from the body." [By being free from the body Porphyry does not mean separated from it, but simply not in bondage to it.] . . .

He repudiates the theory that clairvoyance, prophecy, etc., were the results of the inspiration by external gods, but says that they are a function of the Divine Spirit within man, and that the exercise of this function becomes possible when the soul is put into that condition [attitude] which is necessary to exercise it. The consciousness of man may be centred within or beyond the physical form; and, according to conditions, a man may be, so to say, out of himself or within himself, or in a state in which he is neither wholly without nor within, but enjoys both states at once. . . .

It is said that Porphyry was several times during his prayers leviated into the air, even to the height of ten yards or more, and that on such occasions his body appeared to be surrounded by a golden light [The same thing was true of St. Thomas of Aquin, St. Theresa, and others in the Catholic orders; both the leviation and halo occurred during the contemplative ecstasy of many of the Catholic saints.]

The gods are everywhere, and he whose soul is filled with such a divine influence to the exclusion of lower influences is, for the time being, the god which that influence represents, possessing his attributes and ideas. The nature of the union of the soul with God cannot be intellectually conceived or expressed in words; who accomplishes it is identical with God, he is divinity itself, and there is no difference between him and the latter.

The union of the soul with God is at the same time the union of God with the soul; a very different thing from the other state mentioned above, in which the soul is filled with the influence of *a* god, a being external to himself, by which he becomes for the time being "the god which that influence represents, possessing his attributes and ideas."

This latter is simply the psychometric blending of the subject with another individual soul, who, though above and greater, is yet external to the soul thus magnetically brought, for the time, under the dominating attributes and ideas of the controlling god or spirit, and thus made to personate and give expression to.

This, too, is a very common experience of modern mediumship, the medium when the influence is withdrawn remaining practically unchanged, retaining nothing of the elevation temporarily experienced while in the abnormal condition.

Union with God, on the other hand, is the realization of oneness of life and being with the very essence and nature of the Father in the infinite within; the centre of our being opened as a well-spring in the love, wisdom, and power of the infinite Spirit and universal Being of "our Father in heaven," in whom " we live and move and have our being." This experimentally realized is not temporary experience, but the permanent opening and activity of our own inward life in its conscious blending with the source from which it springs—the supreme and universal life of the Impersonal and Infinite Father—and thus the blending of the Universal Life and Consciousness with ours in its individual development and external activities.

This is an inward experience of personal divine realization, not the taking on temporarily of the attributes and qualities of another being, external to *us*, with which we may be in temporary psychometric rapport, and thus for the time personating and giving expression to as if our own.

It is the actual opening and enlargement of our own individual and personal life, through conscious unity with God in the life, by which we become self-conscious of the spiritual nature, source, and impersonality of our interior and real being. It is the realization by the soul of its own attributes, qualities, and supremacy as spiritual being. It is the coming into its original and true possessions— the glory it had with the Father before the world was.

In that supreme hour of the Christ experience, he said : " And now, O Father, glorify thou me with thine own self, with the glory which I had with Thee before the world was."

This is the high privilege of spiritual realization awaiting all the earth-born children of God, the realization of their own God-nature *as* His children, and when realized the individual has no need of leaning upon anything or anyone that is external to himself, because he realizes the fulness of all being within himself.

Within the depths and heights of his own interior and spiritual being, to which his self-consciousness is now open, he is one with God, and goes forth in his relations with that which is external to himself " in the power of the Spirit," or, with the consciousness of his divine nature and supremacy upon him, as an embodied spiritual being and son of God, the outward and inward planes of consciousness being co-ordinated in experience.

This was the perfectly co-ordinated state of being which characterized the Christ, and which, he assured his followers, was possible to all who really believed and truly followed him. This was the living water which he said he would thus give unto men, of which, if they drank, they would never thirst.

The inspiration and elevation experienced by communion and psychometric sympathy with other souls higher and greater than our own is blessed, and may indeed prove a heavenly ministry and a degree of quickening to the advancement of our own growth and development, but the special elevation to which we were raised by the temporary contact and sympathetic union is gone when the contact is broken. "He that drinketh of this water shall thirst again," said the Christ; "but he that drinketh of the water that I shall give him shall never thirst: for the water that I shall give him, shall be in him a well of water, springing up unto everlasting life."

Sympathetic union with whatever is external to ourselves is necessarily of a temporary character and must end, as it began, in the entire separation of the individual states, if our own permanent individuality is to be maintained: for it is impossible to enter into vital and permanent union with that which is external to us without the total loss of individuality. But, on the other hand, the opening up and expansion of our own inward life by conscious unity of will and spirit with God in the life, by which the outward man in its individuality and relations to environment is co-ordinated with the inward life in the realization of its impersonal union with the Divine and Universal, but enlarges and perfects the individuality in all its external relations and activities.

The gods [continues Porphyry] "are not called down to us by our prayers, but we rise up to them by our holy aspirations and efforts ; we are connected with them by the all embracing power of love."

Jamblichus, a disciple of Porphyry [both Neo-Platonists], says : If the soul rises up to the gods, she becomes godlike, and able to know the *above* and the *below ;* she then obtains the power to heal diseases, to make useful inventions, to institute wise laws. Man has no intuitive power of his own ; his intuition is the result of the connection existing between his soul and the Divine Spirit ; the stronger this union grows [in his consciousness], the greater will be his intuition or spiritual knowledge. Not all the perceptions of the soul are of a divine character ; there are also many images which are the products of the lower activities of the soul in her mixture with material elements. Divine Nature, being the eternal fountain of Life, produces no deceptive images; but if her activity is perverted, such deceptive images may appear. If the mind of man is illumined by the Divine Light, the ethereal vehicle of his soul becomes filled with light and shining. A.D. 333.

"*Proclus* was born in Byzantium, A.D. 412, and died in Athens, A.D. 485. He was a hermetic philosopher and mystic, having often prophetic visions and dreams. It is said that he had the spiritual power of producing rain by his 'prayer,' and of preventing earthquakes. He was very pious and self-denying, and on some occasions his head seemed to be surrounded by a glory of light."

We must now close this interview with the great mystics of the past. Those we have consulted are representatives of their several classes, yet these, it must be remembered, represent but a small number of the many orders that have lived, wrought, and left their impress upon the world. What we have gleaned, however, from the testimony and experience of these earnest students of the interior and higher life, of the great principles involved, and which these serve to illustrate, we shall find of great suggestiveness and help in our own direct study and effort at personal realization. In closing we will call attention to the labors of a great mystic of our own time, but of a different class: one that may very properly be called a mathematical mystic, who, in the study of the human consciousness and its evolution, has reduced its processes literally to geometrical forms, defining the orderly steps of its unfolding with mathematical precision and demonstration.

This mathematical genius finds the geometrical order manifest in the evolution of human consciousness and intelligence perfectly symbolized and prefigured in a corresponding evolution of plant life, as expressed in the geometrical lines, angles, curves, and perfected forms of leaf, flower, and fruit. Hence he illustrates the successive steps and stages involved in the actual evolution of consciousness in man, by beautiful diagrams of this geometrical symbolism found in the leaf, flower, and fruit of plants.

By the positive laws of geometrical development governing both the evolution of plant life and the self-consciousness of man, Mr. Betts, the author of "Geometrical Psychology"—the book to which we refer—has given us what seems to be a perfect mathematical demonstration of the three distinct planes of consciousness legitimate and necessary to the full normal development of man in his relations to the cosmos. And, singularly

APPENDIX. 161

enough, he has given them the very names which we have given in our exposition of these same forms of consciousness, viz., Sense-consciousness, Soul-consciousness, and Spiritual- or God-consciousness.

This is one of the most valuable and important contributions to the scientific formulation of the New Psychology that has yet appeared; because it has a mathematical basis.

To appreciate the force and beauty of his representation, the work itself, with its illustrative diagrams, must be read and studied. We shall quote only so much of his description of the steps and stages involved in the natural evolution of the personal consciousness on these several planes, as will present a fair picture of the same to our students, for the suggestive help it will furnish to the study and mastery of the subject of these Lesson-Helps.

FROM "BETTS' GEOMETRICAL PSYCHOLOGY"—"AN ABSTRACT OF HIS THEORIES AND DIAGRAMS. BY LOUISA S. COOK." (*Geo. Redway*, London.)

Mr. Betts has spent more than twenty years in studying the evolution of Man. He contemplates Man not from the physical, but from the metaphysical, point of view; thus the evolution of Man is for him the evolution of the human consciousness. He attempts to represent the successive stages of this evolution by means of symbolical mathematical forms. These forms represent the course of development of human consciousness from the animal basis, the pure sense-consciousness, to the spiritual or divine consciousness. . . . Mr. Betts felt that consciousness is the only fact that we can study directly, since all other objects of knowledge must be perceived through consciousness.

Mathematical form, he considers, is the first reflection and most pure image of our subjective activity. Then follows number, having a close relation to linear conception. Hence, mathematical form with number supplies the fittest symbols for what Mr. Betts calls "The Science of Representation," the orderly representation by a system of symbolization of the spiritual evolution of life, plane after plane. "Number," Philo said, "is the mediator between the corporeal and the incorporeal." . . .

SCHEME OF EVOLUTION.

Mr. Betts' representative diagrams trace the path of the nomad through five planes or standing-grounds of human evolution. He commences from the animal basis, which he takes as the zero or starting-point of the human scale of progression, and proceeding upward, ends with that culmination of human possibilities when man becomes more than man, and his further evolution must be as a being on such a transcendent plane of existence that it might be called divine.

All attempts to trace the cause of the evolution of life must begin at some point of the eternal circle. Mr. Betts has begun with the evolution of man, but the principles of evolution which he discovers through his studies apply equally to the evolutions of higher or lower forms of consciousness, and even to those planes of existence which we usually term inanimate. Only by studying ourselves, he believes, can we ever arrive at a true knowledge of the external.

The starting-point of the human evolution is the animal sense-consciousness, which, though a positive plane of life for the lower animals, affords but a negative basis of consciousness for man. . . .

The first human standing-ground is that of rational sense-consciousness. Self-gratification is the predominant motive on this ground. . . .

The second standing-ground is negative, the reaction from the first, which is positive. It is the ground of the lower morality. Will is developed as distinguished from the mere impulsive volition of the first ground. Self-control is the predominant motive. The dimensions of the form are contracted to a point which is not now a mere point of possibility as at first, but a focus of realized sensuous activity repressed. Commonly, however, this ground consists rather in the circumscription than suppression of sensuous activity (the total suppression of sensuous activity would be death), which is now no longer allowed exercise for its own sake, but as a means to an end. Thus the representation of forms

APPENDIX. 163

actually possible in life, instead of being a point, will be a circle, or rather a circumference, for it is not necessarily a true circle.

The third standing-ground Mr. Betts calls the ground of spiritual activity, but it is rather psychical than truly spiritual, the spiritual evolution being that of the fifth ground. Work is the motive of this ground. The sensuous activities are now allowed free exercise again, but as servants, not as masters. The representative diagrams are in three dimensions, for the consciousness now has depth as well as surface extension. . . .

The fourth is again a negative standing-ground of life, the reaction from the third ground, as the second from the first. It is the sacrifice of the personal Will, from which sacrifice it is reborn as a spiritual Will, in union with the divine or universal Will. Mr. Betts professes himself unable to give any representation of life on this ground, since even the most advanced of ordinary humanity have scarcely entered upon it; also being a negative and reactionary ground, it would be almost unrepresentable by diagram. The motive of this ground is a yearning for union with the infinite.

The fifth standing-ground is spiritual, the ground of intuitive knowledge. As the spiritual now becomes a positive plane of life it would be capable of representation if we were able to draw diagrams in four dimensions, but our present consciousness is limited to only three. Normal human beings have not yet attained to this plane of life, though the aspirations of a few tend thitherward; consequently no definite conception can be formed of such a condition, except by inference from the analogies and correspondences of lower planes of life or through the revelation of higher beings who have already developed this grade of consciousness in themselves. It is the plane of the occult what we with our limited ideas of nature call the Supernatural. . . .

"That Being must exist," Mr. Betts is obliged to postulate as the first law of evolution. Manifestation is to arise. . . . From the first law that Being shall exist, Mr. Betts deduces the corollary "Being exists in variety." If Infinite Being is to be manifested in finite existence it must be through infinite variation of the finite, for otherwise the cosmos would be a manifestation of monotony, not of infinity.

PRINCIPLES OF REPRESENTATION.

When we contemplate our consciousness—and in the fact that *we* can contemplate consciousness as *ours* lies a proof of the quality of the self which will presently be brought to light in the diagrams—when we contemplate our consciousness we find there one element which differs from all the rest. Whereas *they* are multitudinous, chaotic, changing, it is one, alone, comparatively unchanged. It may be called the undifferentiated differentiation of the One, and all the other elements are related to this substance. We call it "I," the subject of consciousness. The relation of object to subject on the lowest plane is sense; on a higher plane, intellectual faculty; on the highest, knowledge. I see, I think of, I know that I see and think of . . . some object. . . . We feel as if our centre were fixed, and so far as its relation to its own activities are concerned it is fixed. . . .

The first sensation produced by the action of a determinating cause is simple consciousness, the feeling of being alive. To this succeed touch, sight, hearing, taste, and smell; and on the hypothesis of the Septenary law of perfectness, there must still remain the possibility of two latent senses not yet determined.

Every sensation alternates with a pause or blank of non-sensation, the ebb from the state of consciousness to the state of unconsciousness again. . . .

Every conditioning agent, whatever may be its plane of operation, in its ultimate analysis is resolvable into pulsation, vibration. For instance, vibrations within definite limits of velocity cause a determination of consciousness as sensations of Light and Color, other vibrations having a slower rate, sensations of sound, and so for the other senses, in accordance with the law of determination. It is not inconceivable that beings might exist to whose internal activity the external vibrations we call Light and Sound might appear differently, so that the determinant that produces the sensation of sight in us might excite the sense of hearing in them; thus sight would be indeed the "music of the spheres," or with a changed relation again, sound might be visible, as Coleridge pictures in his beautiful fragments of "Kubla Khan:"

"With music loud and long
I would fain build that dome in air,
That sunny dome! those caves of ice!
And all who heard should see them there."

Or there might be beings of ampler development yet who could adjust any sense to any series of vibrations, tuning their instruments, so to speak, to the required pitch.

[See account of the Bertolacci children in Appendix to "The Way, the Truth, and the Life," by the Author. These children, through the opening of the inner senses and their co-ordination with the outer, were enabled to change the focus of their eyes at will, so as "to see the most minute and the most distant objects with the naked eye, as though they were looking at them with a microscope or a telescope."]

If the optic nerve could be related to some force akin to Electricity instead of Light, an immense expansion of the power of vision would accrue, for in Electricity a long line of action takes the place of a point of radiation. Distance would be practically annihilated, as we should be able to receive almost instantaneous optic telegrams of most distant scenes. Some adjustment of this nature may be the explanation of the phenomena of clairvoyance and other of those mysterious inner senses whose existence in no small number of persons it is hardly possible to doubt in face of the constantly increasing mass of evidence.

[The fault with this suggestion is, that its author forgets that the inner senses referred to are related to an inner and vastly more subtle medium of vibratory transmission than that to which the nerves and physical organs of sense are related, and to which the grosser nerve-aura cannot be made to respond. That medium is the psychic ether, and in its instantaneous and far-reaching vibratory action it is, indeed, "akin to Electricity;" and with these inner senses opened and adjusted to this elastic ether, we may "receive practically instantaneous telegrams of most distant scenes." This was demonstrated by the experience of the Bertolacci family, as well as by many others.]

We know through their chemical effects that there are rays of light vibrating more rapidly than the violet rays, which cause us no answering sensation of color. Possibly in the process of evolution, as our determining law enlarges, we may develop the consciousness of new and unknown colors beyond the violet and below the red rays. . . .

The action of the determining agent upon the eye is twofold. It causes the realization of a subjective sensation and of an objective perception. Thus far existence is but a vibratory line, a string of individual isolated instants of consciousness. Such probably is the form of the consciousness of a young infant or of a total idiot—a one dimensional consciousness ; the warp of time is being spun, but not the woof woven with it.

After the repeated recurrence of any sensation, though slightly varying in form, the individual develops the consciousness of its identity and begins to form an image or idea, both of the subjective sensation and of the accompanying objective perception, which he can retain in his mind though the sense affection of which it is the counterpart is transitory. Mr. Betts calls this power of ideation Imagination, using it in the literal sense of the word. As a prism receives a beam of light and deflects the rays, holding them apart so that the colors of the spectrum are separated and distinguished, so Imagination receives the stream of consciousness and holds apart and compares the different experiences. . . . Imagination, according to Mr. Betts, is a polar activity. Besides its positive function of comparison, whereby ideas are held apart and distinguished, it has also the negative function of combining them into a unity, so that we feel the continuity of consciousness to be unknown.

[Space will not allow of further quotation of Mr. Betts' interesting analysis of the nature of consciousness and memory, and the specific conditions of their development, etc., but we must hasten on to his special analysis and description of the five human standing grounds with their three positive planes of consciousness.]

VARIATION.

In the examples of consciousness which have been given, the various undulations of real activity into which the original simple circuit of the ideal activity has been differentiated flow on in a complex rhythm of harmony. There is no impulse left undetermined, no want left unsatisfied, and thus no incentive to further progress, seeing that completeness is already attained, though but of a low order. It is the discord, the conflict of opposites—power struggling with condition and yearning seeking satisfaction—that impel men on toward the realization of a higher plane of existence than consists in personal gratification and the enjoyment of externals.

The original Alpha and Omega forms in their simple perfectness may be taken as the representation of Adam and Eve in the Earthly Paradise—types which are approximately realized in the early youth of every man or every race born under favorable circumstances. The simple savage living amid bountiful Nature feels little or no disproportion between his desires and their fruition. His wants are so few and simple that he can easily gratify them, and the means of gratifying them are at hand. It is true there must be from the first some lurking dissatisfaction with every realization of the ideal, since no realization can exhaust the ideal; and had it been otherwise there could have been no progress. But at first the dissatisfaction is so unrealized that it does not force itself upon the attention ; it lies latent in the consciousness.

 . . . But the perfect type must be broken through, the serpent of dissatisfaction must bring discord into Eden that ultimately a higher perfectness than ignorant innocence may be realized, that of purity [positive virtue], which, knowing good and evil, freely chooses good.

Since Being must exist and can only be manifested in the finite through infinite variation, there must necessarily be in every man some disproportion between his alpha and omega activities, whether of perception or imagination. This disproportion at first leads a man on unconsciously, as he thinks to experience yet greater delights with each new fruition of desire. But as his desires expand, and their gratification is increasingly difficult, the disproportion becomes a conscious element in his existence ; a thrill of unsatisfaction accompanies every determination of activity, even the most pleasurable, impelling to the continuous search in new directions for new and more perfect means of self-gratification, only to be proved in their turn equally unsatisfying. . . .

Imperfect determination causes a hiatus to be felt, which acts as a determinant of consciousness into self-consciousness. The child or the simple savage is self-conscious in that his experiences have relationship to himself. The realization of imperfection causes a further development of self-consciousness in that he now contemplates his experiences as being *his own*. . . .

The limitation which prevents the higher possibilities from being fully realized produces the consciousness of sin and short coming, yet this very limitation is the foundation of the individuality and idosyncrasy of character which on a higher plane render social union and corporate unity possible. But although the one contains the germs for future development, no true brotherhood is possible while the form remains enchained within the circle of self-gratification. It does but oscillate in unstable equilibrium between its conflicting desires. . .

NEGATIVE MORALITY AND ITS MATHEMATICAL EQUIVALENTS.

The second plane or standing-ground of human life being a negative one, a reaction from the first ground of egotism may be passed over briefly, as it is scarcely at all capable of representation by diagram.

The increased strife of conflicting desires, as the counterpart forms expand and their law of development becomes ever more complex and contradictory, causes the consciousness to become more and more self-conscious until the ego is forced to pause in the pursuit of pleasure and contemplates existence itself.

Just as after repeated occurrence of sensations the child or savage begins to identify them and compare them one with another, so now, after a more or less prolonged experience of life on the first standing-ground, the man begins to reflect on his life as a whole and to distinguish its characteristics, except in the case of those persons who remain all their life enchained on the sensuous plane. He compares the reality of his actual life with his ideal, that dim feeling of absolute life that underlies his consciousness and which is his from the fact that the circuit of his life-energy is contained in the great Alpha, the movement of Universal Spirit. His perception awakes to the fact of the delusions and ephemeral character of the life spent in the pursuit of pleasure. He sees that to satisfy his desire of life through the senses is an insoluble infinite problem. The more his thirst of life grows the satisfying waters flow backward from his lips. A revulsion of feeling sets in, and he withdraws his desires from their wonted channels.

At this crisis some, in disgust of life, have committed suicide; others have reduced life to the extremest negation possible short of death. But more commonly the evolution of this ground consists in the circumscription rather than the annihilation of the former activity. The ego, a mere point at first, becomes a focus; its realized activities, concentred and repressed, are allowed to act only within the circumscribing circle. In the "I will not" of renunciation and self control morality begins and the existence first becomes a persistent and independent thing and takes satisfaction in the consciousness of life as life. The mere impulses of volition of the first standing-ground can scarcely be called Will at all, and no morality is possible except as obedience to external law, and no religion is possible except through external revelation, the affirmation of those egoes who have attained a higher stage of progress.

The degree in which the second ground of life is manifested varies very widely in different persons. Some never get beyond the barren negative morality of this ground—"the eternal nay," Carlyle calls it. Life never becomes anything to them but the giving up of pleasure; they never reach "the eternal yea," but instead of passing through death to life, wrap the grave-clothes about them, and remain in the tomb. Others, on the contrary, pass so easily and quickly from an ideal of pleasure to one of duty, and find such happiness in duty, that the renunciation of the lower pleasures is hardly felt at all. . . . Self-conquest becomes easier every time the foe is vanquished.

In the latter stage of evolution of the first ground the form was developed from conflicting scales of progression; owing to this some tendencies will be found to be strong out of due proportion to the rest, and will consequently require a greater exercise of Will to control them; so the form of consciousness on the second plane will not be wholly without personal character. . . .

The motive of life on the second plane is but a kind of inverted egotism. The ego faces itself and admires itself, save only when it disobeys the ascetic law it has imposed upon itself for its own satisfaction. Though self-control lays the foundation of true morality, alone it is but a barren and negative condition, a consciousness of immense powers, with but little result, other than the repressing of the ego's own impulses; consequently it is the negation of life that can only last till the internal, ever increasing through repression, bursts its self-imposed bonds and, surging upward, lands the ego on the shores of the higher morality.

THE EVOLUTION OF THE HIGHER MORALITY: PHILANTHROPY OR ALTRUISM—ITS PRINCIPLES.

The death-in-life of the second standing-ground cannot last. It is but the stage of transition from a lower to a higher one, to which sooner or later there must be an uprising ; for the second ground contains within itself a principle of progress.

The energy of the ego, circumscribed by Will and held in check from its free exercise on the sensuous plane, gains strength by reason of the limitation of its activity, until at length it finds a new outlet for its impulses and leaps upward, rejoicing in a new ideal of life.

As the first ideal was *having* the passion of personal possession, and the second *not having* the first imperfect impulse of sacrifice, now the third becomes *doing* ; and not pleasure, but duty, not self-gratification, but work, is made the aim of life. And virtue is no longer the conforming to an external, but obedience to an internal law. . . .

The circuit of the new activity (every activity is polar) depends upon a point above the form which is conceived of as an absolute and infinite non-ego, for not yet does perception awake to the oneness of the soul, the higher ego with the infinite. The first life-centre represents the personal ego, the self that separates from the All. The second life-centre represents the divine ego, the true individuality that unites with the All. A new determining law comes into operation to which the personal ego voluntarily subordinates his activity, regarding this law of internal determination as the expression of the Divine Will. In some minds it may rather take the form of a vocation to which the life is voluntarily dedicated, or any other form under which the principle of duty and right may be conceived of.

As the desire of the ego required a non-ego, an object as the condition of its fruition on the lower ground, so the desire of the higher life requires a non-ego for its fulfilment. The determinant in this case is not objects, but other egoes. Mankind supplies the necessary complement through which the ideal activity of the ego can be manifested. For the personal aspirations to be realized it must carry others up along with it. Through the needs of humanity the ideal activity of the soul is embodied in a definite form of duty and use. Forms of religion,

APPENDIX.   171

forms of government, ideal arts, benefit institutions, sciences, all the
busy work of the world that is not wholly connected with objects of
sense, are the product of this activity.

The ego as it enters this state of life begins to realize that—

"To dignify the day with deeds of good
And constellate the eve with noble thoughts,
This is to live, and let our lives narrate,
In a new version solemn and sublime,
The grand old legend of humanity."

THE POLAR OPPOSITE FORMS OF THE THIRD GROUND.

. . . The faculties of sense, the rational attributes of the ego,
are no longer compared among themselves, but are all subordinated to
the central idea, and are allowed free exercise as the servants or instruments of the higher life.

This higher life is progressively realized by means of appropriate
determinations. The first blind impulse to do good soon becomes
rationalized in a greater or less measure, probably according pretty
closely with a scale of rationality the ego had developed on the lower
ground. The antithesis of the alpha and omega forms becomes apparent. . . .

Once more there is no undeterminateness manifested in the form.
For a time the ego feels as if in the gladness of the performance of duty
its ideal was being realized.

Frequently not all the life energy of the form is conditioned by the
determinants of duty. In such a case the remaining activity falls back
upon the method of the lower ground and is determined by the law of
pleasure, for since the impulses are inherent impulses they are regarded as the expression of the Divine will, and are allowed free exercise in subordination to the new law, and not held in check as on the
former standing-ground. The essential life of the form is determined
in three dimensions by the law of duty; the superabundant energy is
determined in two dimensions by the law of pleasure, and extends itself outwardly, forming a kind of foliation, a fringe of personal enjoyment, about the true life; . . . and since other egoes are
the usual determinants on this ground, this efflorescence may be taken

as representing an inclination toward social pleasures and recreations. . . .

Just as the impulse of the lower life was progressively realized as the fruition of personal desire in determined forms of intellect and emotion, so now the impulse of the higher life begins to be realized in the alpha and omega forms as the satisfaction of impersonal desire or Love. Duty becomes the objective form, and Conscience the emotion of duty, the subjective form of the consciousness. The external and internal activity of the ego is determined by the altruistic law of determination to virtuous thought and action. In what measure the activity is thus determined, in that same measure the thought and action react upon the ego as Conscience, the faculty of judgment, sifting, examining, and discerning the motives of conduct and relating the action and thought to the ego in the progressive qualification of consciousness. . . .

VARIATION OF THE THIRD STANDING-GROUND.

In the first dawn of the new life and the gladness that accompanies the first exercise of the powers of soul, the ego does not perceive any disproportion between its ideal and the possibility of realizing it. It contemplates the needs of humanity, which are its determinants; the non-ego, through which its ideal of duty is realized; but it is not saddened at the sight of sorrow, and suffering, and ignorance, and want, for they afford a field for the exercise of its powers; it believes that it shall be happy itself and shall make others happy.

If the consciousness is but low in the scale, the determinants are probably the personal needs of those immediately surrounding it. Perhaps it is in the faithful performance of family duties that the ego feels its ideal shall be realized. In a consciousness of a higher order the desire might take the form of becoming a local benefactor. Thence it might expand to patriotism and humanitarian schemes for the good of the nation. In the highest natures the aim would be universal philanthropy, the training and benefiting mankind generally.

The dotted line of activity ascending from the central point, the personal ego, may be regarded as the line of faith and aspiration, the impulse of the higher life which yields itself up to be determined by the law which it feels to be divine. As the activity spreads outward and becomes determined through other egoes a sphere is afforded for the realization of these impulses. But after a time a disproportion begins to manifest itself between the actual possibilities of the ego which is absolutely limited at any particular moment of time and the perfectness of its determining law. If the personal limits be considered as 1, the demand upon it would be 1+ if duty is to be performed as perfectly as conceived of. . . . Consequently it never can perfectly do the thing it would. Some compromise has to be effected between the two. . . . The best actions are seen to fall short of the standard. An incurable sorrow, a sense of sin and failure, accompanies every manifestation of activity. Thus suffering, the great Educator again takes its place as a factor in the evolution. The disposition between the ideal and the real again forces itself upon the consciousness. . . . The conflict within him at last compels man to contemplate life on this plane as a whole, and the ever-widening disproportion he perceives between his powers and possibilities again impels him on toward a higher plane. He perceives that not in philanthropic work. not in intellectual thought, not in personal virtue, shall his ideal become realized. The blooming corolla of fiery activity fades and perishes, shrivelling away into an unsightly rag, and man is left once more, heart-sick and bereft of all, to seek, if so be he may find it, the way of life and truth. . . .

SPECULATIONS ON A FOURTH DIMENSION IN SPACE.

. . . Suppose a man were able to reverse the poles of his attention and make what was positive negative and what was negative positive, it is conceivable that he might not see this material world and look at . . . something else, . . . and if so, what? Since three dimensions exhaust the limits of extension it can be conceived that he might see space in three dimensions again, but space of an opposite quality to that with which he is habitually familiar.

In the occasional accidental occurrence of second sight and other interior senses in some of the phenomena of Spiritualism; in the traces of genuine Occultism which may be found in the literature, especially the sacred literature, of all nations and times we have any record of, we have evidence of the possibility of such an alternative space-perception of seeing, hearing, etc., in a world not perceptible to the ordinary senses. In the language of Occultism the five subtle senses with which we perceive the more interior quality of space are called the astral senses—*i.e.*, clairvoyance, clair-audience, and touch, taste, and smell on the astral or etherial plane of matter. . . .

With a consciousness of space in alternating three dimensional spheres alternately cognized through the exterior and interior senses, we might infer as a mathematical certainty the existence of a fourth dimension in space, although the direct perception of it might still be impossible to us. . . . The possibility of such a projection of the consciousness into and out of spheres constitutes the stage of human evolution which Mr. Betts calls the fourth standing-ground. But the actual realization of a four-dimensional state of consciousness belongs to the fifth ground, which is the positive ground of life, whereas the fourth is only a negative and intermediate one.

THE FOURTH STANDING-GROUND OF LIFE.

. . . The fourth standing-ground of life, like the second, is a negative and reactionary one, the alternation from an objective to a subjective stage of evolution. . . .

On the third standing-ground the consciousness had dimly felt the presence of another plane of life than the physical. By the time the fourth ground is attained the psychical or astral plane becomes a possible object of direct perception. The attention can be directed to or withdrawn from either plane. The interior senses are developed as the foundation of the higher evolution, as the exterior senses were developed as the foundation of the lower evolution; and as the lower sense was subordinated to intellectual perception, so the psychic sense becomes the tool of the spiritual perception of the fifth ground. But on the fourth ground, although the psychic sense may, and indeed must, exist, and consequently the consciousness is intermediate between a three- and a four-dimensional development, being able to cognize either sensuous or supersensuous objects, yet the ego feels to have no impulse for the exercise of either sense. The hope of realizing his ideal through work has faded, and again he lies at the "centre of indifference," again he hears the "everlasting nay."

The third ground was a fruitless attempt of the ego to realize its ideal by work, undertaken with and for humanity. The impulses were determined by a power seemingly external, which was regarded as the Divine Will. In the first gush of the ascending activity, when the life burst forth into flower, it seemed as though perfect satisfaction was to be gained on this plane, but as the evolution proceeded, undeterminateness, deep-seated as the root of life, became increasingly manifest. An element of failure accompanied even approximate success. Imperfection was found to mingle with effort of usefulness. An ever-widening chasm yawned between the apparent possibility and the actual accomplishment. The refuge in action failed. Reaction set in again, and the corolla that bloomed so brightly faded and withered away. . . .

The personality was progressively developed on the earlier standing-grounds of life and culminated on the third, but neither in personal pleasure nor in personal virtue was the ego able to realize its ideal. The fourth ground may be considered as the evolution of negative impersonality. The third ground was a state of busy activity, of doing. The fourth is a state of sorrowful passivity, of not doing, because the desire is no longer to the act, though action continues mechanically, because virtue has become instinctive. It may be summed up in one word—sacrifice. The ego has given itself up, the personal desires are quenched, and the whole desire of the soul is poured forth in a deepening cry for knowledge [enlightenment], life.

Desire completes fruition, and when the soul, from the depth of its sorrow and despair, flings itself forth into the infinite in an infinite passion of longing, then when the battle of life seems lost, all is won. Spiritual perception awakes and the isolated fragment is received back into the bosom of the All. In the self-forgetfulness of that supreme moment, in the unutterable bliss of that reunion, the sacrifice is accomplished, the self-surrender is complete. Man passes through the gate of death into the only true life, which is not egotism, not altruism, but eternal unity. This transition has been variously called Regeneration, the new Birth, the Beatific vision, Union with the Logos, the threshold of Nirvana.

THE FIFTH STANDING-GROUND OF LIFE.

In the reaction of the second ground the point or focus had the content of the plane—*i.e.*, the activities of the sense life. In the reaction of the fourth ground the point or focus has the content of the sphere, the entire physical, intellectual, and moral nature, for reason and virtue have become instinctive, as natural to man as his breathing or the beating of his heart.

As in the transition to the third standing-ground of life the sense-perception of the physical ego became the servant, the instrument, of the psychic ego, so now in the evolution of the fifth standing-ground the metaphysical and ethical perception of the psychic ego, which have now developed their appropriate organs, become the servants and instruments of the higher ego—the machinery, so to speak, of the spiritual ego, the true being, the I *am*, which, as it begins to be recognized as the true self, makes man more than man, for it is a ray of the great *I Am*, the unposited point which is everywhere and in All. The evolution of the first ground is Having or Egotism, of the third is Doing or Altruism. The evolution of the fifth ground, the culmination of Humanity, is Being or Unity. The three grades of consciousness might be called sense-consciousness, soul-consciousness, and spirit or god-consciousness.

But though point after point of knowledge has been won, though realms of ignorance have been enlightened, and numberless barriers of indolence have been overthrown; though the individual ego has perceived its oneness with the All, first by faith through revelation on the earlier grounds of life, next by reason through inference as its intellectual faculties expanded on the third ground, and at last by actual perception through the purified and exalted faculties of the higher self as the fifth ground was reached; yet ever beyond the actual point—however elevated the position it has attained, and however extended the circumference embraced by consciousness—lies the unposited point, the Great Unscrutable. The finite cannot compass the infinite. The lesser alpha, the individual being, though its identity of substance with the great Alpha, the All-being, be disclosed, yet still exists within the circumscribing circle of Prakriti. Consciously one with the All in substance, it remains consciously separate from the All in form. But since the limit of Prakriti, the infinite Omega, is not an actual but an ideal limit, within which the actual limits of each form may be for ever and ever extended, there lies before the ego the possibility of eternal progress, through ever-heightening cycles of objective manifestation, alternating by reason of polarity with ever intenser states of subjectivity. And herein lies the joy and glory of existence, for were it not so, were there fixed a hard and fast limit beyond which none could pass, that would be annihilation. Life would culminate in death, Hope be quenched in Despair, and Existence, instead of an everlasting progress toward Light, would become the blank darkness of desolation.

While we remain enchained by our personalities on the lower planes of life, scarcely can the imagination prefigure, in faintest outline even, the mysteries of so transcendent a plane of life. As the first ground was compared to the leaf and the third to the flower, so this may be called the season of the fruit, and the fruit has the seed of life in itself and is therefore immortal.

On the fourth ground man becomes negatively impressional, on the fifth he becomes positively impressional, for he recognizes his personality as not himself, but one particular expression of the forces of Nature. He does not act—that is, his personality does not act for its own sake, for he has passed the stage of personal doing, impelled by personal desire. He does not act, but Nature acts in and through him, for he has become a conscious part of Nature, and can read her runes and knows her laws. He has power over matter, for all things are himself, diverse manifestations of the One. He has influence over men, for all men are himself, diverse fragments of the great $I\,Am$. He draws all men up with him, for though he has crossed the threshold of the New Life himself, not until all men have entered into it with him can the unity be fully consummated by the union of humanity in a common subjective life—a life in which, though the centre of consciousness of each remains unchanged, the circumference embraces the consciousness of all mankind, the four-dimensional unity of the individual spheres of consciousness. . . .

No representation is possible of the form of consciousness on the fifth standing-ground of life, although it would be representable if we were able to conceive of it. . . .

Mr. Betts expects that his theoretical Science of Representation will be complemented by a practical Science of Determination, for he believes that every natural form is a symbol, and if we understood the mystic inscriptions of Nature we might read in every natural form some word of Life.

A Science of Determination would be the foundation of a true system of sociology, in which each form of human kind would take its natural rank in a great spiritual hierarchy. . . . He considers his Science of Representation to be the Alpha Science, and that the complementary

Science of Determination will be chiefly the task of women to develop it. . . .

A brief abstract like the present one can give but a meagre conception of Mr. Betts' Theories and Diagrams. It will have served its purpose if it shows that the studies which Mr. Betts has made toward developing a Science of Representation make clear the possibility of using mathematics as the handmaid of metaphysical as well as physical science. . . . Mr. Betts puts forth his work as the first step in a new direction, or at least the first taken in that direction in our day, and he hopes that others abler than himself may follow in the same path and geometrize the laws of the universe more successfully than he has done.

EXTRACTS FROM LETTERS IN APPENDIX (BETTS).

This frail attempt to solve the problem of life may seem unmeaning, but when we come to understand that all life is an undulatory activity, and that color is an infinite array of varying undulations, it may perhaps expand into real insight by our tracing the various and infinite permutations of this principle through all states and conditions of existence in the Garden of Eden, whose flowers are human beings, and thus we get back to that Garden from which our ancestor was so abruptly expelled. . . .

Only after close study and almost endless experiment does light suddenly burst in upon the subject. When such occurs I have always felt and invariably acknowledged that the flesh has come from a higher world. But without the study and experiments I feel sure (I have proved it also) that no light would come. [A study of Du Prels' "Philosophy of Mysticism" will convince the student that these sudden flashes of light on hidden things come from the interior and higher planes of consciousness of our own transcendental ego, opened for the moment to self-consciousness by the abstract condition into which the soul had fallen through deep interior meditation. The external observation had fastened the attention and interest upon the problem involved, which led to interior meditation and this to the momentary opening of the higher consciousness and its intuitive perception of truth. The glad recognition of the truth by the self-consciousness awakes the personal ego to itself again in the joy of possession, and the door of the deeper impersonal life, which is identified with truth, is closed. This again is a powerful hint pointing to devout meditation, prayer, and contemplation on things of the impersonal and divine life, as the true and certain means of opening the higher planes of consciousness and bringing the external into co-ordination therewith.] Mr. Betts continues: The idea was and is "I and Thou." How to explain this and thereby to explain everything was my problem, for I placed this as the central idea of existence, the second part of the "I Am that I Am."

It seems to me the great want in the present day is a practical view of life, for you cannot call that life which does not live, and if all could see a symbol of their life in every flower that grows (a true symbol, as I have been trying to show) they would probably soon see more beauty in life than they had done. And if to this the *sudden* knowledge should come of the hidden unity of all, what a ground would they find for living outgoing activity! . . .

It may be that here and there a distinguished pure soul (already belonging to a higher sphere) obtains entrance into the highest, but what about the multitude that has to plod the road thither, concerning whom not one is to be lost? We have invented steam-engines to transport the body with speed, and telegraphs to wing our words, but what spiritual engines have yet been thought out to speed the soul upward ? . . . [We trust the student will find that desideratum met in the specific method of induction disclosed in these lessons. Had the mystic fathers understood the three planes of consciousness in their normal reciprocal relations, and held the ideal of the permanent opening of the transcendental planes and their normal co ordination with the external and sense-plane in the body instead of the ideal of salvation in a future life, upon which their whole attention and desire were fastened, they would have then solved the problem for all future generations. This they have left for us to accomplish, and let us be faithful to the work thus bequeathed to us, grateful for what they did ; while recognizing their limitations and misdirected efforts, let us complete and perfect what they so grandly began.] . . . This is not a poetical term it is Science, when I repeat Love is the *Substance* of all things, the reactionary activity of the Intelligence, the solid substratum of the Objective Universe ; this, too, is not a figure of speech, but an all-embracing reality, which gives to existence its eternal standing-ground and unites all together, so that we think we see the same world, hear the same sounds, walk the same path, clasp the same hands, when reason tells us it cannot be so, but each invents or produces that which it thinks, and the centre of all our communication is the hidden pavilion of Absolute Being. This is clearing the ground for the apprehension of the fact that the movements of celestial bodies are.the thinking products of a personal intelligence in advance of terrestrial forms. . . .

I have often stated that I was not looking for leaves or flowers when I commenced my studies, and the coincidence of their forms with the laws of representation struck me as very remarkable, and then it at length became clear that these forms have all along been showing to us the secret which all have been trying to arrive at, viz., the laws of Being manifested in existence. . . . For Wisdom and Love are the two counterparts toward which all are tending, and their apotheosis is not of to-day, but forever.

www.ingramcontent.com/pod-product-compliance
Lightning Source LLC
Chambersburg PA
CBHW031439160426
43195CB00010BB/784